Private Sector Development in Egypt

Private Sector Development in Egypt

Edited by
Marcelo M. Giugale
Hamed Mobarak

The American University in Cairo Press

Dar el Kutub No. 8839/95
ISBN 977 424 376 5

Library of Congress cataloging-in-publication data:

95-961314

Private sector development in Egypt / edited by Marcelo M. Giugale, Hamed Mobarak. — [Cairo] : The American University in Cairo Press, 1996.
p.
I. Giugale, Marcelo. II. Mobarak, Hamed

Printed in Egypt at International Press

Contents

Tables

Tables

Preface

On October 9 and 10, 1994, a landmark was crossed in modern Egyptian economic history. During those two days, the government of Egypt, in partnership with the largest local business associations, and with support from the international donor community, held the country's first private–public Private Sector Development (PSD) Conference. The event marked the coming of age of an ongoing economic reform effort, as it explicitly signaled the common goal of abandoning a centrally planned development model in favor of a market-driven, private-sector–led strategy.

The conference brought together national and international expertise, private agents and civil servants, producers, traders and financiers, official donors and nongovernmental organizations, the public in general, and the media. The business associations prepared and presented position papers that articulated their views on how specific, actual PSD constraints should be dealt with. A World Bank report was also issued identifying those constraints, and mapping out forthcoming PSD challenges. Key lectures were delivered. Illuminating floor debates took place. And a PSD Steering Committee was created after the conference as a permanent mechanism for private–public policy dialogue.

But the conference's main achievement lay less in its outstanding technical contribution than in its fostering of country awareness, commitment, and ownership of the PSD agenda. To the outsider, the meeting was a fine symbol of a nation openly acknowledging its economic problems, candidly discussing solutions, and eagerly seeking to learn from successful international experiences.

This volume is an attempt to record and disseminate the conference's achievements. It brings together selected, edited proceedings, focusing primarily on self-standing, analytical contributions. Its core objective is to provoke further thinking on Egypt's PSD issues in as large an audience as possible. Its publication has been commissioned by the PSD Steering Committee, and has been made possible through resource contributions by the Committee's Secretariat and the World Bank.

Thanks are due to a large number of participants. In the first place, to His Excellency Dr. Atef Ebeid, Minister of Public Enterprise Sector and Minister of State for Administrative Development and Environment, for envisioning the potential for, and leading the execution of, close private–public policy dialogue in Egypt. Special thanks are also due to the local thematic Task Forces that articulated the Egyptian private sector's views. These Task Forces were sponsored by the Alexandrian Businessmen's Association; the American Chamber of Commerce in Egypt; the Egyptian Businessmen's Association; the Federation of Egyptian Industries; and the Federation of Egyptian Chambers of Commerce. Important inputs were also received from the Egyptian Federation of Labor Unions and from the Egyptian Banks Federation. The World Bank, USAID-Cairo, and UNDP-Egypt provided financial and human resources for the conference organization. Mazen Nagi, Enrique Mayor-Mora, and Yassin Mobarak ably coordinated the book's production.

Introduction: The Rationale for Private Sector Development in Egypt

Marcelo Giugale and Hamed Mubarak

WHY PRIVATE SECTOR DEVELOPMENT IS IMPORTANT FOR EGYPT

Over the past five years, the Egyptian government has undertaken an economic reform and structural adjustment program that has achieved remarkable results in terms of macroeconomic stabilization and relative price connection. Up-front financial liberalization and a gradual removal of trade barriers were also implemented. The program has also included policies that aim to improve the regulatory environment for enterprises, mainly by discontinuing price controls, relaxing industrial investment licensing procedures, and removing the legal biases favoring public sector companies. The latter have been reorganized as an initial step toward their privatization. In 1993, the reform program entered a second phase, where further adjustments in key relative prices, a deepening of the trade and financial markets reform, the broadening of the public sector restructuring and privatization processes, and additional improvements in the regulatory system were all put on the policy agenda.

In essence, Egypt's economic reform initiative amounts to moving from a centrally planned, public-sector-dominated economy toward a competitive, market-based one in which the private sector is to play the leading role. The objective is to achieve rapid, efficient, and sustainable growth—something that the past centrally-planned model has not delivered. By fostering private sector development (PSD), it is expected that the living standard of Egyptians, especially that of the poor, will be raised to its potential. In other words, PSD is the core tool in the country's new development strategy.

But why should there be a change in development strategy at all? PSD is neither simple nor costless. Does Egypt really need to speed up its economic growth through PSD? And, if so, does it need to speed it up now? Can't PSD wait?

The answer to those questions lies in the economic and social challenges facing Egypt over the next decade.[1] First, even in an optimistic scenario in terms of migration, female participation in the labor markets, and public employment reductions, halving Egypt's current unemployment level by the year 2000 will require the creation of five million new, private jobs between now and the end of the decade. That is about eight times as many jobs as the local private sector created during the whole 1976–86 period (when the economy was growing relatively fast) and a 50 percent increase over the private employment level at the beginning of the current economic reform program. This picture is further complicated by a major market mismatch in Egypt's education system: public "technical" secondary schools currently turn out seven times more graduates (about 400,000 per annum) than would be needed even if the non-agricultural private sector was growing fast (that is, at about 10 percent per year). Not surprisingly, then, 70 percent of the officially unemployed are 19 years old or younger, and 60 percent hold an intermediate degree or higher.

Second, about six million Egyptians are ultrapoor, that is, have an income lower than a third of the national average. These Egyptians live on a quarter of a dollar a day or less. The poor are characterized by larger and younger households with a high incidence of disability and malnutrition, higher mortality and morbidity rates, little or no access to basic infrastructure (like safe water and sanitation), and a high degree of geographical concentration in Upper Egypt (40 percent of Egypt's poor live there, although the region comprises only 30 percent of the country's population). A skewed pattern of income distribution aggravates the situation; the income of the richest twenty percent of the population is six times higher than that of the poorest twenty percent, a pattern that is more unequal than that of Bangladesh, Ghana, India, Indonesia, or the Philippines.

Third, growth of the kind that will deliver a major alleviation of the unemployment and poverty situations will require a major investment effort. Yet, reduction in public sector investment is a key element in the stabilization component of Egypt's reform program (central and local government investment as percentage of GDP is projected to fall by about 10 percent over the next five years). Also, investments by state-owned enterprises (SOEs) will be limited along the road to privatization; no new business expansions by SOEs will take place. Overall, then, the public sector's investment as a percentage of GDP will probably shrink by a quarter during the 1990s. It will be up to the private sector to fill that vacuum; but what kind of private investment growth is involved in that objective? The answer naturally depends on the expected (or desired) output growth path. For instance, to sustain a rather moderate average level of real growth (3.5 percent per annum) and a modest improvement in standards of living (i.e., real private per capita consumption increasing by about 1.5 percent per annum), private investment would have to more than double in real terms between now and the year 2000. Put in perspective, private investment would have to grow twice as fast as it did during the boom years (fiscal years 1975 to 1983), when real GDP growth averaged 9 percent per annum. And that assumes a major improvement in investment efficiency (incremental capital output ratios falling by about 50 percent).[2]

Finally, to achieve fast growth, Egypt will need to absorb foreign resources (e.g., raw materials, capital goods, know-how)—something that, in turn, will call for a sustainable flow of foreign currency. However, Egypt is a country of chronic trade deficits (food imports are larger than all non-oil goods exports taken together). Although workers' remittances, the Suez Canal, oil, tourism, and foreign aid have traditionally provided for most of the country's foreign cash needs, they are likely to prove insufficient if Egypt's economic growth speeds up (and might themselves experience long-term decline in line with regional geopolitical developments). This poses a major challenge in terms of private export performance. For instance, even assuming that the level of public sector non-oil merchandise exports remains constant (an unlikely prospect as the public sector's role in the economy shrinks), private sector non-oil merchandise exports would have to increase sixfold from their current level for the balance of payments' current account deficit to remain, say, below 2.5 percent of GDP by the year 2000.

The four challenges described above—unemployment, poverty, investment, and exports—point to the need for fast, outward-oriented, job-generating, private-sector-led growth as the key to eliminating poverty in Egypt within, say, one generation, and, ultimately, as the standard by which the success of the reform effort will be measured. But can the Egyptian private sector deliver that kind of growth? What are the impediments that should be removed for that to happen?

This paper argues that the real constraint on PSD in Egypt is the lack of a conducive business environment, an umbrella concept that embraces the mix of legal, regulatory, institutional, financial, tax, technological, and human resource parameters within which individuals find incentive for (or disincentive to) creative entrepreneurship. In this view, those parameters are closely interrelated and are critical as a whole. That is, policy intervention to remove single impediments is bound to deliver little private sector response. Comprehensiveness is essential to PSD. From a policy-making point of view, however, the issue is one of prioritization. What minimum subset of impediments could be tackled to unleash PSD in Egypt?

THE ELEMENTS OF A CONDUCIVE BUSINESS ENVIRONMENT FOR EGYPT

This section describes the core, current impediments to PSD in Egypt. It is not meant to be thorough; a detailed analysis of most of the listed constraints is provided by the area-specific chapters of this book. Instead, we provide here a factual overview and a brief explanation of why and how those constraints dampen private sector initiative.

An adequate macroeconomic framework

A sound macroeconomic policy environment will be needed if private-sector-led growth is to succeed in Egypt. The maintenance of fiscal, monetary, and exchange rate policies that promote financial stability and an externally sustainable growth path are required. In addition, the efficient allocation of resources, furthered through an open trade regime, and the fostering of saving and investment, attainable through an effective tax system, will be required.

The status of the commercial judicial system

Enforceable property rights and commercial contracts are at the very foundation of a free market economy. As the number of private transactions has grown (along with the attendant litigation), the Egyptian commercial judicial system has proved to be slow, expensive, and uncertain. Since 1987 the annual caseload has increased by half. The average commercial case takes six years to be decided. Using the current rates of filing and disposition, there will be 26 million cases awaiting resolution in the courts by the year 2000. This is equivalent to eight thousand cases per judge. It is therefore obvious that an overhaul of the country's commercial judicial system, which was initially designed to serve a planned socialist economy, is needed if private-sector-led growth is to succeed.

The system has two main deficiencies. First, it is badly in need of additional, qualified judges. Several compounding factors have led to this: judges' caseloads are too heavy; they lack the specialization needed to render a technically proper decision; their low wages makes it difficult to train and retain them; and the system of promotion is based more on seniority than performance. Furthermore, the lack of qualified and motivated support staff and the poor infrastructure facilities for case management add to the woes.

Second, the judicial system, even by developing-country standards, is grossly underfunded. In addition, its services are inefficiently priced. The cost of commercial judicial decisions is extremely high as, in effect, the commercial system has been designed to cross-subsidize criminal justice.

The approach to business tax administration

At the heart of efficient business tax administration lies predictability and transparency. This is not the case in Egypt, where the arbitrariness and ambiguousness of the process actually deters potential investors, especially foreign ones. Within this system, incentives granted by the government to foster private investment, such as tax holidays, are rendered meaningless as their benefits are outweighed by the tax uncertainty. The arbitrariness in assessing taxes has resulted in lower-than-potential corporate tax receipts, a serious matter for a country that relies on them twice as heavily as the OECD average.

The fundamental problem of Egypt's business tax administration system lies in the conditions that provide the tax collectors with virtually unlimited discretionary powers. These conditions include lack of independent tax appeal mechanisms, no legally recognized accounting standard, and the practice of rewarding collectors according to the revenues they bring in. In this context, tax collectors can (and do) unilaterally assess the taxpayers' liability, instead of auditing their declaration. It is not surprising, then, that an estimated half of all taxpayers seek (or accept) informal settlements. As a result, the government collects less tax revenue than would otherwise be forthcoming and creates a major barrier to private investment as large corporations tend to shy away from projects with uncertain tax costs.

The government's policy of universal auditing has added further uncertainty to business tax administration. The bureaucratic pressures of universal auditing, combined with a five-year limit on claims by the tax authorities, has resulted in the frequent use of unfounded claims by the collectors before the five years elapse in order to trigger a second five-year period of tax inspection. In the end, a business may not know how much tax it has to pay ten years after accrual.

Demand–supply imbalances in the market for skilled labor

The current undersupply of skilled labor for the Egyptian private sector is due, in great part, to the educational policies implemented during four decades of central planning. Education and training in public technical and vocational postsecondary institutes and specialized technical secondary schools focused in the areas that were a priority for a public-sector-led growth strategy. Working for the public sector, apprenticing in the informal private sector, or migrating abroad were the only ways to develop market-worthy skills. As private sector development has pushed forward, private sector demand for skilled labor has remained unsatisfied as the public provision of skills is inadequate and the alternative sources insufficient.

There are two main barriers to skill building in Egypt—the market insensitivity of the public technical secondary schools and the fact that the private sector is not participating in the formal training process. The technical secondary schools currently produce seven times more graduates than what the market is demanding. Even assuming an unrealistically optimistic private sector growth scenario, it will take about twenty years to absorb the existing pool of job-seeking technicians. Furthermore, the skills learned in these institutions are of little or no use for small enterprises, the only sector in which unsatisfied demand for formally trained technicians exists.

The public sector effectively dominates Egypt's formal training process. This is happening for a number of reasons: the reluctance of larger firms to make long-term human capital investments in an environment that is not yet business friendly; the predominance of small and micro enterprises (SMEs) which do not have the resources for training; and the limited trainability of workers given their weak general education base (half the labor force is illiterate).

The technological status of the private sector

As economic reforms proceed and growth is sought through the private sector, the issue of the technological competitiveness of Egyptian firms will become critical. Whether or not Egyptian firms will be able to compete internationally will depend on the speed with which they will be able to identify, absorb, and exploit new technologies.

So what are the constraints Egypt faces in this respect? Central planning's legacy has been such that the country's most advanced technologies were (and to a great extent still are) concentrated in the hands of the public sector which, under poor management and no competition, used them inefficiently. The private sector in turn was left with technologically simple and primarily resource-based activities behind high import barriers.

Currently, there exists a supply-driven approach to technological development in Egypt. Public organizations operate in technology identification, extension services, standards and metrology, and research. Given the large externalities involved in the technological area, it is not uncommon for the public sector to intervene. However, in the case of Egypt, there needs to be a greater 'awareness' link between the private sector's needs and the public sector's services. If economic growth within the context of PSD is to be achieved, then the public technology institutions must consider private participation on their boards, financial autonomy, aggressive marketing strategies, adequate individual incentives, and updated physical infrastructure.

Furthermore, the prohibition to the full operation of foreign-owned international trading houses (a major source of technology transfer), inadequate tax incentives for private R&D, lack of long-term financing or venture capital for technological upgrading or development, a legal framework for intellectual property protection that has only recently been brought up to standards, and a limited quality-skills base are all additional factors stifling technological advancement in Egypt.

High transaction costs for private exports

Economic reform is shifting the source of economic growth in Egypt from the public to the private sector. However, for the private sector to provide long-term sustainable growth, it will require growing access to international markets. Accordingly, the success of the country's reform program will depend on the elimination of policy distortions that unnecessarily raise the transaction costs and, thus, effectively price the private sector firms out of the international market.

Nowhere are those distortions more perverse to exports than in the availability and cost of imported inputs. As Egypt is a country with limited natural resources and technology, it relies heavily on foreign inputs. High import tariff (and nontariff) barriers make those inputs particularly expensive. Also, for a number of legal, institutional, and administrative reasons, the compensatory mechanisms (drawback, temporary admissions, free zones) do not work properly.

Two crucial items that add to the cost of exports originate from the legacy of central planning. First, all major export infrastructures (ports, airports, transportation networks, shipping agencies, etc.) are in the hands of the government, are demand insensitive, and are monopolistically priced. Second, several government institutions have simultaneous jurisdiction in terms of inspection, certification, quality control, approval, licensing, and levying—all cost-increasing and time-consuming activities of doubtful usefulness.

These distortions not only increase the financial cost of exporting goods from Egypt but also greatly reduce the ability of Egyptian firms to cater quickly to the latest consumption trends, where the value added is likely to be higher. Nor can Egyptian exporters compete with faster delivering suppliers from other countries. In an increasingly integrated international market, where speed has become a necessity in the export market, Egyptian exporters are presently handicapped.

Size-specific constraints on small enterprises

Small and micro enterprises (SMEs) play a critical role in Egypt's economy; they represent 98 percent of private economic units, provide over three-quarters of private jobs, and produce an estimated 80 percent of the country's private value added. Yet despite being a leading player in PSD efforts and employment opportunities, they still face critical size-specific constraints: they lack capital to pay for the sunk, start-up cost imposed by the existing regulatory system, and they have virtually no access to legal physical space, formal credit, or markets.

Egyptian small-sector firms usually locate in violation of urban planning codes, as environmental and health concerns prohibit them from operating in cities. Setting up shop in the New Industrial Zones (with tax holidays and subsidized land prices) is not feasible in practice, as the system of allocation of land excludes small-sector firms which lack the institutional mass needed to see their applications through the governorates' investment approval committees. In fact, even if they do succeed in getting land, they are usually unable to obtain the establishment and operations license, a requirement originally meant to guarantee industrial safety but in practice used to assure compliance with all other regulations. The alternative, renting, is less than perfect: rent control laws have long discouraged investments in the shops-for-lease business.

Formal financing for SMEs is not forthcoming either. The fundamental reasons lie in the banks' lack of institutional capacity to identify, appraise, and supervise small-scale project lending (as a result of four decades of administratively allocated credit); a lack of incentives for the lending institutions to search for new markets (as barriers to competition in banking still exist); and the crowding-out of more sustainable market-priced private initiatives (as the government and its donor agencies provide subsidized lending schemes to SMEs).

Finally, Egyptian small enterprises have little access to markets. This is due to three main reasons: prohibition to the operation of foreign-owned international trading companies; predominance of public firms in the marketing and distribution networks; and government procurement procedures that are de facto impenetrable to small firms.

Availability of long-term finance

The Egyptian private sector has little access to long-term financing. The three core long-term instruments for corporate finance are still underdeveloped—long-term credit, a securities market, and leasing.

Egypt's gradual approach to economic adjustment has fostered uncertainty in the banking sector. In such circumstances, it is not surprising that banks have been reluctant to undertake long-term commitments or to develop the necessary appraisal capacity. Lack of competition in the banking sector has compounded the problem, primarily via the dominant role of public banks, the de facto freeze in new bank licenses, high capital requirements for entry, and the prohibition of controlling ownership by foreigners.

Although recently improved, the securities market remains essentially a restricted option for private enterprises as a source of long-term finance. This is due mainly to five factors that hamper market liquidity and investors' confidence: 1) most stocks are closed to public trading (usually through rights of first refusal embedded in the corporate charter of the issuing company); 2) direct price regulation by the Capital Market Authority; 3) inadequate disclosure standards; 4) poor procedures for approving, executing, and settling transactions; and 5) regulatory restrictions on bond issues.

Egypt's potential for leasing, as an indirect source of long-term finance, remains mixed. On the one hand, Egypt has a generous system of tax holidays that provides plenty of opportunities for leasing, as well as a new, forthcoming legal framework for financial leasing. On the other hand, the present status of the commercial judicial system limits the speed with which leased equipment can be repossessed in the event of default, and the complicated system of tax administration may not be flexible and transparent enough for tax-motivated leasing deals to occur.

AN OVERVIEW OF THIS BOOK

Private sector development will be as critical for Egypt's economic future as it will be difficult to achieve. This thought sets the stage for the rest of this book. In what follows, individual contributions focus on both strategic aspects of PSD, as well as on specific, sectoral constraints.

Regarding development strategy, the role of the government in a private-sector-led economy is analyzed in the chapter by the Egyptian Businessmen's Association. This is then supplemented by the American Chamber of Commerce in Egypt's contribution on the role of the private sector. Taken together, the main message from these two chapters is: let the private sector, through market competition, take the lead in economic activity, and limit the government to market failures and public goods. This probably means a smaller Egyptian government, but certainly not a weaker one; a common theme of both chapters is that PSD needs a predictable framework of enforced law. Caio Koch-Weser's article makes this point from a regional perspective—the potential for Middle East peace will be realized only when accompanied by the kind of faster, sustainable economic development that the private sector can deliver when allowed to compete for profit and when public policy is limited to the provision of a sustainable macroeconomic environment, a business-friendly regulatory system, and a mechanism to share the fruits of growth across all parts of society.

Eight of the chapters present constraint-specific analysis. Ibrahim Shihata highlights the uncertainties brought about by inconsistencies in the country's legal and judicial systems, and provides specific examples of legislation that heightens business risk.

Labor laws are analyzed in Hussein Ibrachy's article; his emphasis is on labor mobility, especially on firing and hiring rules. His proposals seek to achieve a balance between corporate productivity, job security, and social stability.

Tax laws and administration are thoroughly reviewed by Hazem Hassan; he shows how transparently administered, growth- and saving-fostering tax reform could go hand in hand with fiscal balance in Egypt.

Finance is tackled by the American Chamber of Commerce in Egypt. National saving patterns, as well as financial intermediation, institutions, tools, and markets are all examined. Specific policy solutions are proposed, with two main themes in mind: to avoid distortions in the choice of saving channels, and to maximize competition (and innovation) in the provision of financial services.

An urgent call to link Egypt with the international markets is made by the Federation of the Egyptian Chambers of Commerce. A more open trade regime and a foreign-friendly foreign direct investment (FDI) environment are seen as the key vehicles for that. Reduction in the levels and dispersion of import tariffs; removal of nontariff barriers to trade (especially those of a bureaucratic type); demonopolization of currently public infrastructure; and the relaxation of the rules governing foreign investment are, among others, the focus of the recommended policy reforms.

The conditions under which the industrialization of Egypt could take place are the subject of the Federation of Egyptian Industries' chapter. The Federation argues that the continuous dominant role of the public sector in industry, the barriers to market entry and exit, the lack of antitrust mechanisms (for both public and private monopolies), the poor quality and high price of state-run infrastructure services, and the intrusiveness of the regulatory environment all combine to diminish Egypt's opportunities for internationally competitive industrialization (especially in post-Uruguay Round world trade).

Finally, size-specific constraints to the growth of SMEs are discussed by the Alexandrian Businessmen's Association. Policy recommendations are put forward to deal with those enterprises' restricted access to formal finance, physical space, and markets. Related, successful international and local experiences of intervention are analyzed.

1 For a detailed technical analysis of those challenges, see *Private Sector Development in Egypt—The Status and the Challenges*, World Bank, 1994, prepared for the conference "Private Sector Development in Egypt: Investing in the Future," Cairo, October 9–10, 1994.

2 Ibid.

One

The Role of the Government

The Egyptian Businessmen's Association

THE PRIVATE SECTOR'S ROLE IN DEVELOPMENT

The Egyptian private sector has witnessed impressive growth in its share in economic development. Following the 1961 nationalizations, the public sector became dominant and was controlled by a rigid system of centralized planning and inefficient management. The country's first full-scale economic plan, 1960–65, proved relatively successful, but between 1967 and 1973, growth averaged only about 3 percent per year. Since then, a continuous effort to move Egypt away from centralized economic policy has been implemented. The 1982–87 plan concentrated on improving Egypt's infrastructure; the 1987–92 plan emphasized economic reform, including an increased role for the private sector. The current National Plan emphasizes expanding the role of the private sector, which is now responsible for 61 percent of the country's GDP.

Egypt is now passing through a transitional period. Its political, economic, and social systems cannot be separated from global developments. It has become necessary for Egypt to be more outward-oriented, to cope with liberalization of the global economy by giving more support to its private sector. As a consequence, private investment is gradually increasing—expansion, new projects, and reinvestment of net profits are taking place on a large scale in various industries. Table 1-1 illustrates that the performance of the private sector in the national GDP (fiscal year 1992/93) outweighed that of the public sector.

Economic reform in Egypt

Since 1987, the Egyptian government has pursued a comprehensive program aimed at reforming and restructuring the Egyptian economy. The program encompasses major areas of economic activity, including financial and foreign exchange activities, trade liberalization, public

Table 1-1
Public and private sector shares of the GDP 1992–93

	Public	Private	Total	Weight (%)
	(value in LE millions)			
Total Commodity Sectors	24,856	41,544	66,400	49.50
Total Production Service Sectors	16,894	27,966	44,860	33.40
Total Social Services Sectors	10,395	12,600	22,995	17.10
Gross Domestic Product	52,145	82,110	134,255	100.00

sector reform and privatization, and price and investment deregulation. The program was supported by substantial debt relief from the international donor community, Gulf War-related financial assistance, and international financial institutions. Restraint in government spending and new sources of revenue have lowered the budget deficit from approximately LE17 billion in 1990/91 to LE5.3 billion in 1992/93. The government has begun to focus on structural reform issues such as privatization, liberalization of trade and tariff regimes, and deregulation; only limited progress, however, has been achieved.

Measures to alleviate the impact of reform on low income groups and to increase labor mobility and reallocation include a limited annual wage increase as well as the creation of the Social Fund for Development, financed through donations, loans, and government contributions.

Private sector strategies for improving the Egyptian economy

An assessment of resources available to the private sector shows that Egypt enjoys many advantages over other countries of similar levels of economic development such as individual initiative (or the willingness to take risk), often called entrepreneurial spirit; effective management techniques; sufficient sources of finance capital; abundant skilled labor; geographic position; established international business contacts; modern communications/information systems; and access to state-of-the-art technology.

Mobilization of resources to increase future investment

The private sector must effectively utilize the resources mentioned above in order to achieve development goals, specifically to create nearly 5 million job opportunities over the next five years and increase Egyptian exports. This could be accomplished by: 1) creating a proper environment to attract private investment and free enterprise to participate in the development process; 2) abolishing bureaucratic and other impediments hindering access to resources; 3) opening other economic sectors to the private sector to allow for opportunities to effectively use resources; 4) providing incentives in taxes, customs, and so forth; 5) encouraging reinvestment of surplus; and 6) encouraging the private sector to develop its research and development (R&D) capabilities in order to set criteria for creating advanced technology, assemble a pool of Egyptian scientific know-how, and support labor intensive investment.

Employment of resources for the privatization process

Considering the successes of reform in Egypt so far, it is obvious that the best avenue to development is an injection of private sector investment into the economy. Instead of going through the whole foundation process of an investment, priority should be given to private participation in state-owned enterprises (SOEs). This will help accelerate structural reform, improve the quality of the national wealth, achieve efficient utilization of resources, and finally, mobilize economic resources at large, consequently creating job opportunities and contributing to the alleviation of unemployment. Almost by definition, the private sector's role must be maximized in the privatization process.

Additionally, there are other measures and policies that would help to facilitate the pursuit of privatization. The stock exchange should be strengthened to increase its ability to attract capital investment by individuals and companies. Privatized companies should be exempt from taxes for an appropriate period of time, with an emphasis on the restructuring phase, and the 40 percent duties paid on sales of assets should be eliminated. Economic criteria for evaluation of SOEs should be established and Egyptian expertise should be recruited. The role of the banking system in assisting investors and buyers should be increased, with an emphasis on selling SOEs and alleviating debt problems; simultaneously, a flexible program for reallocation of excess labor should be applied. The government should broaden privatization to all sectors, especially services such as telecommunications, mass transportation, power generation, maritime activities, mass media, and so forth. A public awareness program should be devised to dispel misunderstanding about privatization, which is not merely the selling of SOEs to private individuals, institutions, companies or banks; rather, it is a general framework to best utilize the available facilities and assets of SOEs. It aims to gear them toward increased economic and social responsibilities, and to attain the maximum economic return on investment.

Case studies of other countries privatizing their economy have confirmed that directing private capital and private management to increase the efficiency of the SOEs' performance stimulated the national economy. The government will gain an increased income from taxes on the future profits on those SOEs. In the meantime, the government will not share the losses. Along with increasing the capability of the government to pay debts, privatization is a means for proper and fair distribution of the ownership of national wealth.

Globalization of Egypt's private sector

Egypt's external environment is encouraging and is gradually moving toward closer cooperation with the international community. Egypt needs to move beyond domestic markets and develop an international role, with the private sector playing a major part. The strategy of involvement in the international arena and accommodation of new rules and trends are of such necessity that assistance is required.

Many countries face the dilemma of whether to follow a strategy of economies of scale to satisfy local markets or economies of scale that adopt international market standards. The experiences of other countries shows that globalization succeeds in fostering production of goods and services with global demand, which are both internationally and locally competitive.

The private sector is contributing in this context by developing business opportunities and strengthening trade and investment relations with foreign counterparts. Among the major fields of cooperation are: the establishment of joint ventures in different economic fields, primarily industry, tourism, construction, agriculture, and services; the opening of markets for Egyptian products and services, with emphasis on labor intensive projects; the acquisition and accumulation of needed technology and know-how; cooperation between Egyptian and international companies in third markets; the familiarization of Egyptian producers with international quality standards in order to upgrade Egyptian products and services; and integrating the Egyptian capital market with its international counterparts.

THE ROLE OF THE GOVERNMENT

Within the framework of a liberal economic regime, the government has a strategic role of assistance in accomplishing the creation of jobs and the increase of exports. The state should divest itself of ownership, management, and production roles. It is in this context that the role of the Egyptian government in two major areas will be highlighted—specifically, the market forces and the means to improve the efficiency of its bureaucracy.

Market forces

Redefining the role of the government within a framework of liberal economic policy should help to create an organized, stable environment for economic activities. It should initiate policies designed to preserve market forces and to assure fair competition among all production sectors. Incentive systems should be applied to encourage job creation and export expansion. Incentives could be in the form of tax exemptions, provision of land at cost, or exemption from customs duties for those who implement labor intensive product lines and projects.

Government awareness and commitment to this role is fundamental for the success of economic reform. Thus, leadership at all levels, both legislative and executive, must change its relationship with investors and the public to one which is service-oriented, rather than a superior/inferior–oriented relationship. It must develop a closer working relationship with the business community, based on the exchange of experiences and management techniques. This will enhance the use of scarce national resources. It should minimize its role in the production and service sectors. Nevertheless, the government may play a vital role in cases where either the private sector is incapable of providing supply, or where strategic and/or security considerations come into play.

The government and the private sector should collaborate in the preparation and execution of all national economic and social development strategies. Review of constitutional provisions that require change is needed to help implement a truly liberal economic policy. Strategies should be implemented transferring the burden of financing public services directly to their actual beneficiaries. Consumer protection legislation urgently needs to be enacted.

Restructuring the role of government does not mean cancellation of its basic and essential responsibilities and obligations, including management of financial and monetary policies; management of infrastructure investments and services; establishment of policies and provision of means capable of achieving welfare and social benefit commitments, such as social security and public health; assurance of national security and defense; development of an educational policy which serves national goals; fighting corruption; protection of the environment; and organization (without intervention) of the relationships between all national sectors. All these activities are borne from the notion: "Government rules, but does not own; organizes, but does not manage."

Government bureaucracy

The government should decrease bureaucracy and consider reducing the number of existing ministries. Coordination of proper relations among ministries is urgently required. The number of ministries has reached thirty-four. Perhaps these ministries were vital to the former centrally planned system; under a liberal economic regime, however, ministries can be restructured to cope with new methods and realities, based on strategic planning, enforcement of laws and regulations, coordination between government departments, and ultimately, the protection of the public interest. Therefore, its recommended to amalgamate and restructure the duties and responsibilities among the existing ministries.

An administrative reform program should be developed to complement current economic reform. Such a program would protect public interests and rights and would help to achieve an appropriate quality of service. Reform should incorporate careful selection of leadership and expertise capable of responsible administration. Choice should be based on merit and efficiency, not rank or seniority. Government recruitment should be frozen and early retirements encouraged through attractive incentives. Recruitment should target highly qualified Egyptian expertise living abroad. Efficiency and training programs should be instituted at all levels of government. Wage scales and policies should be restructured and tough penalties to fight corruption should be implemented. Finally, to help soften the impact of all this reform, the performance of the Social Fund should be improved, and the role of the private sector in the Fund should be intensified.

The role of government in research and development should be strengthened and incentives encouraging creativity and innovation should be designed. The government should make all research results available and provide assistance in acquiring technology finance from international institutions.

COOPERATION BETWEEN THE GOVERNMENT AND THE PRIVATE SECTOR

The previously discussed issues highlight the roles of the private sector and the government. There are, however, other national issues that can be resolved only through the joint effort of all parties. The experiences of many countries, including European Community nations following World War II and more recently those of the Far East, have demonstrated that comprehensive understanding and cooperation between government and the private sector are essential to achieve rapid development.

Privatization

Since 1961, the Egyptian government has retained almost complete control over economic activities. However, it has been experiencing mounting difficulties. Although privatization is proceeding in the right direction, it still lacks the commitment and bureaucratic resolve required for change, which has translated to a snail-paced process. There is a need for cooperation between the private sector and government to determine and remove impediments to privatization.

Evaluations of SOEs is one of the primary obstacles to their sale; SOEs reject values suggested by consultants. As a result, the Ministry of Public Enterprise has allowed SOEs to evaluate themselves, leading to inaccurate assessments. Profitability should not be the criteria for selling the SOEs. Unprofitable companies could be sold to the private sector or to creditors, after determining fair market value and debt value. Proceeds from sales should be used in servicing debts after rescheduling and, if necessary, in compensating labor. Some shares of profitable companies should be offered on the stock exchange, while the rest could be sold directly to private investors.

Hidden unemployment (unproductive manpower), accumulated in state-owned enterprises, is a heavy burden on the government. This problem requires immediate attention. There are a number of measures that would begin to address the problem in a serious, thoughtful manner—for example, classifying labor and retaining the efficient and productive groups, reallocating special skills to other areas, and encouraging small-scale projects by granting soft loans and facilities through the Social Fund and banks.

Debts of public sector companies constitute a major obstacle to privatization. This could be resolved by partial payment of debts from the proceeds of selling SOEs. The price offered for public sector companies is considered the main factor for decisions on sales by the government. Factors other than price should have priority—for example, rehabilitation plans, retention of existing labor, expansion of production lines, job creation, and so forth.

Unemployment

Unemployment is one of Egypt's greatest socio-economic problems, hovering between 17 percent and 20 percent. Again, this problem requires cooperation between the private sector and government. Unemployment in Egypt is due to a variety of reasons. Chief among them are the lack of investments in projects to create new job opportunities, particularly, investments in agriculture and industry, and the rising costs of job creation due to inflation—for example, the cost of creating a single job opportunity increased from LE 44,000 to LE 60,000 between 1988 and 1993.

The recession that has gripped the nation for several years has resulted in grossly overstocked inventories and has deterred investors from launching new projects, the combination of which has resulted in the doubling of the unemployment rate. The growing number of new entrants into the labor force, a natural outcome of overpopulation, reached a 3.5 percent rate of growth between 1986 and 1992. The government's assumption that it can absorb the unemployed by recruitment into SOEs and government departments is incorrect. It has created the problem of unproductive manpower, that is, hidden unemployment.

Environment

The private sector and the Egyptian government now realize that environmental decay is a cause of a great concern. The 1994 environment law provides the authorities with the mandate to enforce standards and to request environmental impact studies prior to the approval of industrial and tourist projects. The environment itself is a resource requiring protection. A public awareness program on environmental issues and pollution should be adopted. Environmental studies should be included in the Egyptian educational curriculum.

Cooperation with international institutions should be encouraged to acquire the most up-to-date technology to help reduce pollution. Incentive programs for enterprises in environmental projects should be established. This should be accompanied by serious legislation to protect resources and ensure the utmost benefit from funds and programs directed to environmental projects. The government should coordinate between conflicting interests of various sectors, such as industry, oil, tourism, transportation, and so forth.

Information systems

Information is synonymous with democracy; its liberalization will have to come in phases and be based on both strengthening its institutions and privatizing its activities. Liberalization of regulations would be a good place to start—for example, replacing the present procedures of obtaining the approval of the Central Agency for Public Mobilization and Statistics (CAPMAS) for each field research. Registration of the consultancy firms and other frequent users on a one-time or periodic basis should be implemented. Controls on the contents of publications (presently under the jurisdiction of CAPMAS and National Security) should be replaced. Intellectual property protection laws should be enforced. The government should organize and allow easier access to information collected by its agencies and ministries, much of it crucial to the development of Egypt's economy.

Regulatory institutions should be strengthened to enforce companies' obligation to regularly publish their data, and access facilitate to it should be facilitated; simultaneously, general accounting practices should be overhauled and enforced. Government organizations in charge of handling information should be upgraded to include training of civil servants and public education programs. An awareness program should be launched to identify and resolve problems hindering the development of information services. Local media should be upgraded especially to include improved coverage of economic issues and activities. Additionally, a public awareness/promotion component should be included in all socio-economic development programs funded by aid donors.

Government agencies should not be involved in managing information services. Information services would be best performed within the private sector structure. It is unfair for government to compete with the private sector by supplying free or subsidized services like CAPMAS, Trade Net, or Trade Point. Foreign aid programs designed to implement missing information links in the Egyptian economic structure should be tendered among private sector organizations instead of being channeled to government agencies, or used to create additional parastatal structures. Forums for cooperation between local (Egyptian) and international nongovernmental organizations, conducive to developing regional information tools, databases, new channels of communications, and so forth should be organized.

Education

The government has recently taken serious steps toward educational reform in Egypt; however, this reform is still not enough. Fundamental reform should encompass both syllabi and the means by which lessons are instilled into students. Reform of syllabi and teaching methods must be coupled with a healthy environment. A prerequisite for achieving this is the provision of proper buildings, proper laboratories, and proper athletic facilities, and a dramatic improvement in the wages of teachers. These needs cannot be fulfilled by the current education budget.

The elimination of illiteracy is a universally acknowledged goal; there is no such thing as a productive society where illiteracy prevails. Free education for all at intermediate and secondary levels should be supplied; but at the university level, it should be supplied only for the academically outstanding. Nevertheless, this should not preclude encouraging private intermediate, secondary, and technical schools, and universities.

This leads us to an important principle in education which, unfortunately, Egypt now lacks but must develop; specifically, the linking of educational policies with society's demand for areas of specialization. It is evident that the current educational policy seeks merely to find the easiest way to provide enough basic education for each student to move from level to level; this is regardless of the academic and practical abilities. The result is poor standards of education and enormous numbers of graduates whose degrees are not commensurate with the actual needs of local and export labor markets. These markets need graduates specializing in fields ignored or yet to be fully developed under the current system.

SECTORAL ANALYSIS

The following presents the experience of the private sector over the last two decades, and it is meant to highlight the major impediments encountered. Recommendations and suggestions are given relative to each sector's impediments. We believe that all national sectors—i.e., public, private, and government—should collaborate to formulate and execute solutions.

Industry

There has been great interest in developing the Egyptian industrial sector, and to establish its niche on the world economic map with regard to competitive performance. There should be a review of Egypt's industrial strategy, which in the past aimed at achieving local market self-sufficiency and decreasing imports. That was deemed necessary under the policy of import substitution. However, the new policy should depend on industrial development based on advanced technology in order to compete locally and internationally.

It is important to concentrate on comparative advantages characterizing the Egyptian economy, particularly in industry. This would strengthen the ability to compete in local markets without being undercut by imports. This will also increase the competitiveness of Egyptian products in foreign markets. The achievement of these ends requires utilization of low-cost labor and the encouragement and provision of incentives for labor intensive industries to help alleviate unemployment. On the educational end, special education curricula geared toward industrial needs should be developed; skills in sophisticated (high tech) industries should be acquired and accumulated; and Total Quality Management and ISO 9000 systems should be implemented.

In addition, this new strategy should involve the direction of industrial investment to rural and remote areas. This supports economic growth and regional distribution of national income and will help solve socio-political problems arising from urban unemployment. Parallel to this strategy, complete diagnostic sector studies should be conducted on Egyptian industries. These studies should focus on comparative and competitive advantages. Diagnostic studies should be conducted on the textile, power, electronics, automobile, chemical, leather, metal, mining, food, and engineering industries.

A task force should be formed by the Ministry of Industry and its departments as well as representatives of the business community. The task force should be authorized to outline a strategy for industry and to develop major sectors. This would also insure an ongoing dialogue between industrialists and government authorities. The role of the Ministry of Industry should be to support manufacturers and protect their interests vis-à-vis other ministries and authorities.

Flexible incentive systems should be applied to industrial investment projects. The current incentive system provided by Law 159 and Law 230 should be changed. The proposed system should be based on national socio-economic criteria, i.e., export-oriented industry, labor intensive industry, the introduction of advanced technology, and most importantly, projects to rural and remote areas.

Research and development, technological capabilities, and training programs should all be improved. The Ministry of Industry owns and operates twelve research and training centers established in cooperation with the United Nations Industrial Development Organization (UNIDO) (for example, the food industry research center, electronic industry research center, etc.). These centers should be restructured and/or rehabilitated. Participation in their rehabilitation and management programs should be opened to the private sector.

Current quality control measures and standards are insufficient for international competition of Egyptian manufactures, or for consumer safety. This is partially due to unfair competition in the form of dumping policies, especially of low quality products. Therefore, a strict standardization policy should be designed and enforced against dumping and against potentially harmful products, both imported and domestic.

A project concerning subcontracting was proposed several years ago by UNIDO. It aimed to establish information centers to coordinate between European and Egyptian companies which export industrial components. In spite of successes in Tunisia, Morocco, and Jordan, it has not been given much attention in Egypt. Collaboration between the private sector and the Ministry of Industry is crucial to its implementation and success.

GATT has provided some developing countries, including Egypt, with the advantage of industrial protection for a limited period of time. Thus, it is important to make use of this opportunity. The primary means of protection are quota systems, reduced customs duties on unfinished products and raw materials, phased reduction of (or selective) subsidies, restrictions on dumping, and other similar measures

Agriculture

The deepest economic reform so far has taken place in agriculture, a sector accounting for 17 percent of the GDP (fiscal year 1992/93) and 36 percent of employment nationwide. For further progress, both the government and the private sector must consider horizontal and vertical agricultural expansion. Horizontal expansion deals with the actual practice and immediate needs of the practitioner such as water, loans, land, and so forth. Vertical expansion, on the other hand, deals with the infrastructure needed to spark and sustain horizontal expansion such as laboratories, agro-processing, agro-trading, technology, and educational institutions.

Water supply and the related impediments are possibly the most important issue concerning Egypt's long-term survival. Egypt's share of Nile water is 55 billion cubic meters. This is insufficient to meet

Egypt's needs if consumption continues increasing at its present pace. Measures need to be taken to alleviate the current crisis and avoid an impending disaster. Efforts must be made to determine potential new sources and utilize available artesian water resources.

Advanced irrigation systems should be promoted when possible and conservation measures should be mandatory and strictly enforced concerning water consumption. The environmental and economic efficiency of growing traditional crops such as sugar cane and rice, which consume huge amounts of water, should be studied to determine whether it would be more economical to import such products. Again, the environmental and economic efficiency of diverting scarce fresh water for aquaculture projects, versus utilizing sea and lake water, is very questionable. Serious conservation of water from all sources is needed if horizontal expansion is to be achieved in agriculture.

Water is not Egypt's only challenge in this sector; agricultural research and land reclamation are two sides of the same coin which complement each other. Egypt needs to learn from the experiences of others in soil analysis projects to help combat deficiencies in reclaimed land. Fertilization and pest control methods should be upgraded through the use and development of biological methods and technologies to eliminate the use of harmful agrochemicals. It is essential to prevent the transfer of traditional fertilizers from the Nile valley to newly reclaimed areas. Advanced irrigation systems should be introduced to rationalize water consumption and eventually reduce reclamation costs. Profitable nontraditional crops—such as asparagus, grapes, and kiwi—which can penetrate foreign markets, should be introduced in newly reclaimed land.

Up-to-date agriculture machinery should be procured, as should modern means of transportation and warehousing to fill the need created by newly reclaimed land. Basic infrastructure such as roads, power generation, and telecommunications are vital to the success of reclamation plans. Access to soft and low-interest loans available for new land reclamation projects, taking into account the slow return on investment of such projects, should be assured. And lastly, fallow land within the Delta and Nile valley areas should be reclaimed.

Vertical expansion is more closely interrelated with human resource development. Various departments for scientific research should collaborate to develop new methods and practices to boost agricultural productivity, decrease costs, and upgrade quality. There is much to learn from the experiences of others. The latest developments in technology should be monitored through cultural counselors or scientific counselors in Egyptian embassies in Japan, the United States, Western Europe, the Far East, and other centers of research. For quality research to be conducted in Egypt, there is an urgent need for laboratories for soil analysis, plant disease research, and horticulture and water management, to name a few research fields. These research facilities should be available for applied research and be accessible to all sectors of society.

The effects of horizontal and vertical expansion will be to significantly increase export of agricultural products in the long term. To achieve such expansion, full mobilization of resources available to farmers and producers is needed and must be carefully managed. Associations or boards of farmers could be established as "profit-center" entities with the goal of exporting their respective crops. The objectives of such entities would be to provide special intermediate products directed toward re-exportation, support research and development in agricultural fields, develop export strategies and implement them, support international marketing and promotional programs geared to penetrate global markets, and assist in securing soft loans to grow export crops.

Transportation

Preparation and packaging is considered the first step in transportation operations. It is the responsibility of the production company and the shipping company. Both must adopt up-to-date technology to protect commodities from loss or damage during shipping. Preparation of shipping documents is the joint responsibility of the commodity owner, shipping agency, and bank. There is a need to encourage the creation of private nonvessel-operating companies who have the authorization to issue shipment documents, thereby saving time and effort. Also, a system of consolidation which facilitates decreasing the shipment costs of small lot sizes by collecting them with other similar-sized shipments and issuing collective documents should be implemented. Compounding the problems involved in shipping, there is a shortage in warehouse and other facilities at ports of entry. The private sector should be allowed to own and operate port facilities, parallel to, and in fair competition with, state-owned services. Banks should apply the same criteria to all requests for financing of such facilities.

Customs clearance for exports and imports is a process involving a great deal of bureaucratic red tape and regulation from agencies such as the customs department, shipping companies, clearance agencies, and so forth. To streamline customs clearance, the government should organize and regulate clearance agencies, in order to improve the quality of services, and at the same time upgrade the skills and classify existing operators. The Ministry of Finance and the Customs Department must increase the efficiency of their employees and initiate training programs. The Ministry of Finance and the Customs Department should expand the use of computers to simplify and speed up the customs procedures.

For all these measures to be effective, however, the private sector must establish efficient, specialized customs clearance agencies to provide proper services. The private sector should be permitted and encouraged to engage in commodity handling, including shipping, warehousing, loading and unloading, and transportation inside ports. Services provided for ports by the privâte sector would be regulated and quality standards instituted. Furthermore, firms involved in maritime activities should be permitted to lease platform space inside ports.

To encourage private sector investment in the transportation industry, there should be exemptions on vehicles and ships from customs duties in a similar fashion as that granted to aircraft. Laws and associated buying and selling procedures for ships under the Egyptian flag should be revised. Currently, investors are not permitted to use foreign financial institutions to buy or lease Egyptian ships. The establishment of shipping lines connecting Egyptian ports with regional and global markets should be encouraged.

Maritime representation is based on representing the ship owner and handling his business in cooperation with the concerned parties in the embarking ports. Private sector activities in maritime representation have been limited since 1962 to ships up to four hundred tons. The government should allow the private sector to compete on an equal basis with public sector companies in representing ship owners, regardless of the tonnage of ships. This would help to achieve improvements in the standards and efficiency of maritime services, ultimately increasing demand for Egyptian harbors and facilities; also, it would meet the basic request of ship owners to be able to choose their own maritime representative.

Importation

Importation is one of the most influential factors in the Egyptian economy, due to its effects on the national balance of payment. There is no objection to imposing quality inspections on food imports and other perishable commodities. Quality minimums and standards imposed by various ministries (that is, economy, health, agriculture, housing, interior, and so on) are also acceptable; however, the current standardization measures do not protect local industry or consumers. These measures allow unfair competition from imported products. A sectoral diagnostic study is urgently needed to set new standards complying with international market ones and to cope with emerging international trade policies.

Tourism

By the next decade, most international economic reports forecast that tourism will be a major industry in the world economic arena. Tourism not only involves the transportation of people and groups, but also provides a strong stimulus to other sectors of the economy. Tourism requires the support of many sectors including industry, agriculture, national and international services, and so forth. There is still no official specification or recognition of the role tourism will play in the national economy after the year 2000. The articulation of this role is important, as it will determine objectives and tasks for all concerned parties, to guide them in the right direction. Tourism in Egypt requires a "master plan" specifying available tourist areas that could be developed. The master plan would determine the relative importance of each subsector and assure coordination with other sectors including, industry, petroleum, agriculture, and services. Tourism requires flexible liberal bureaucracy in order to prosper. Coordination is required between available tourism resources (especially infrastructure facilities and human resources) and the expansion of such activity. The growth rate of the tourist industry should not exceed 10 percent to 12 percent per annum, so as to avoid an unbalanced relation between supply and demand.

Since tourism is an international economic activity and not exclusively local, avenues for new local and foreign investments should be opened wide. Tourism should be privatized. This would facilitate more rapid and efficient utilization of advanced management techniques and technology. Also, by the twenty-first century, wilderness environments (open deserts, desert mountains, aquaparks, unspoiled beaches, etc.) will be a basic element attracting tourism; thus, Egypt must preserve and prudently develop its environmental resources.

Construction

The share of the construction sector in Egypt's national development plan is, for whatever reasons, usually around 45 percent of total investment. It is therefore vital that impediments in this sector be removed as quickly as possible. The following are some of these impediments, and suggested solutions for them to enhance the performance of the sector. First, technology in all construction systems should be raised to international standards, especially in management and labor training. Second, international systems should be used by Egyptian contracting companies to rapidly initiate joint ventures with foreign counterparts. Third, there should be a focus on construction services exported to foreign markets, especially Africa and the Middle East. Fourth, integration and cooperation between consulting and contracting sectors should be intensified. Fifth, preference to Egyptian contractors in public tenders is urgently required, particularly since the liberalization of the construction market in Egypt. Sixth, current laws, regulations, and licensing requirements and procedures should be revised. Seventh, an insurance system against noncommercial risk should be developed. And lastly, retroactive sales tax on contracts made prior to issuance of new decrees should be eliminated.

Two

The Role of the Private Sector

The American Chamber of Commerce in Egypt

BASIC CONCEPTS, RESPONSIBILITIES, AND BOUNDARIES

The private sector is a profit-maximizing, opportunity-seeking economic agent that responds to market and regulatory signals and endeavors to be technically and managerially efficient to the extent necessary for it to compete. Worldwide and in Egypt, the evidence is conclusive as to the exceptional allocative efficiency of the private sector, which improves with higher levels of contestability in the environment within which it invests and operates. These private sector attributes put the government in the position of the rule-setting agent with the pivotal responsibility of protecting the public's interest, promoting social equity, providing an optimal macroeconomic incentive structure that induces efficient performance, and creating an enabling institutional environment. In effect, the behavior of the private sector as an economic agent is a result of the government-installed institutional and economic incentive systems.

The role of government, according to the neoclassical view, includes being responsible for macroeconomic stabilization, regulation, correction of market failures, and equitable redistribution of income and wealth. In more recent revisions of this view, another role has been given to governments in both developed and developing countries—intervention with the goal of 'catching up.' The proponents of this role draw lessons from the experiences of Far Eastern countries like Japan and later Korea, Malaysia, Singapore, and so forth, which succeeded in the second half of this century in achieving rapid economic and social development. The role of the government in these countries was instrumental in their development success.

Central to this success was a handful of selective government interventions including targeting subsidies to some industries, imposing some financial repression to increase profits and retained earnings, granting limited-term import substitution protection, investing in applied research, rewarding achievement of export targets for firms and industries, developing export marketing institutions, ensuring equitable growth opportunities (termed by President Suharto of Indonesia as "economic democracy"), and a wide sharing of information between the public and private sectors. Today, further evidence in support of government intervention to assume the 'catching up' role is found in countries with developed economies such as the United States, where government investment programs in technology extension centers and national export strategies are being drawn up.

The development recipe of the Far Eastern countries was a combination of a strong surge in domestic private investment and a rigorous improvement of human capital. But in addition to country-specific cultural attributes and favorable world economic circumstances at the time, there are some very important qualifications to the interventionist role of the government that made the East Asian 'miracle' possible: the institutional/regulatory environment took to heart the role of the private sector and promoted domestic and international competition; price distortions were kept to a minimum; macroeconomic management was unusually good; and sector policies focused on productivity growth. Perhaps the most key qualification of all was the presence of an efficient government apparatus that was capable of equitably executing 'surgical' interventions.

The evidence from these success stories shows that the chosen role of the government was one that was concerned with enabling the private sector. The government made critical interventions only with a view to catching up with international competition. These interventions were brief and did not go as far as granting the government the dominant role in investment, output, trade, or employment.

THE CASE AND THE ISSUES IN EGYPT TODAY

The contributions of both the government and the private sector in the Egyptian economy are best understood by examining four questions: What are the boundaries of public/private participation in economic activity? Are the macroeconomic and regulatory environments conducive to private sector efficiency and growth? How is the Egyptian government required to intervene to promote private sector development? And how effective are the existing government and private institutions in advancing private enterprise interests?

The boundaries of public/private participation

In Egypt the playing field of the private sector in terms of investment, production, trade, employment, and so forth, while slowly expanding, is still very small and begins where the boundaries of the government end. Until very recently the government barred the private sector from entering many sectors. A number of them are now readily open for private investment, but many remain either completely, de facto, closed or very tightly controlled by the government—for example, infrastructure, power, trade, transportation, finance, insurance, education, and health. Although the private sector has been legally allowed to participate in about 80 percent of the economy, the government/public sector remains the dominant participant. The sectors which are relatively easy to enter by the private sector constitute less than a quarter of the country's gross domestic product (GDP), excluding agriculture, which is predominantly private.

Across-boundary joint ventures between state-owned and private enterprises organized under investment Law 43, and later under Law 230, accounted for an estimated 10 percent of private investments, or 40 percent of large-scale private investment during the period from 1975 to 1988. Many of these ventures served only to reinforce the dominance of the state's role in the productive sectors. Today, discrimination against private enterprises in favor of state-owned ones has been removed. Policies such as protection, priority in allocating foreign exchange, favorable credit terms, and monopoly access to certain sources of funds have been discontinued. There is no doubt that to a large extent the playing field has become more even. But the boundary in terms of controlling ownership of existing assets and share in new investment has yet to shift. There also remains a number of public sector monopolies in industry, services, and infrastructure.

The macroeconomic environment

Three elements are paramount for the creation of a macroeconomic environment conducive to private-sector-led development: stability, transparency, and sustainability. These elements lead to greater confidence in the business environment. In 1990, the Egyptian gov-

Table 2-1
Share of the private sector in the Egyptian economy (percentage)

	1982–83	1991–92
Investment	40	46
excluding agriculture	41	46
Output	53	61
excluding agriculture	33	45
Employment	65	67
excluding agriculture	23	36
Exports (non-oil)	5	46
excluding agriculture	–	45
Imports	2	20

Source: Central Bank of Egypt

Table 2-2
Private sector share in investment and output 1992–93 (percentage)

	Investment		Output	
	Private sector share	Share of total	Private sector share	Share of total
Agriculture	45	8	98	16
Industry	49	22	58	16
Petroleum (w/ joint ventures)	89	13	17	10
Electricity	0	6	0	2
Construction	56	12	70	5
Transportation	13	5	48	11
Trade, finance, and insurance	73	2	79	20
Hotels and restaurants	91	3	84	2
Real estate	97	12	94	2
Public utilities	0	8	0	7
Education	10	3	7	2
Health	10	2	4	3
Other personal services	4	4	90	5
Total	46	100	61	100

Source: Central Bank of Egypt

ernment launched an economic reform program which took great strides toward macroeconomic stabilization and structural adjustment. The far-reaching Economic Reform and Structural Adjustment Program (ERSAP) has been, by all standards, a successful one, and was implemented wisely and prudently. The ERSAP is now in its second phase (ERSAP II) and has as its main objective supporting rapid and sustainable private-sector-led growth.

Among the numerous achievements of the ERSAP was the reduction of Egypt's fiscal deficit from 17 percent to about 4 percent of the

GDP between 1991 and 1994, and the reduction of inflation from 20 percent in 1991 to less than 8 percent at present. Containing inflation was all the more remarkable as it occurred despite a process of broad price liberalization and deregulation. The prices of most goods and services were completely freed and those of a few others which remained administered, such as pharmaceutical products, were raised closer to market levels. This movement toward price adjustment was accompanied by a gradual liberalization of trade. Dispersion of import tariff rates was brought down to the 5 percent to 70 percent range and all quotas and import bans, with a very few exceptions, were removed.

Of no less importance are the adjustments in the country's financial sector, such as the removal of interest rate ceilings and foreign exchange controls; the discontinuation of the system of administrative credit allocation; the use of market-based instruments (treasury bills) to manage liquidity; and the elimination of restrictions on international capital mobility. In addition, Law 95 of 1993 was passed to allow for a transparent and a more efficient functioning of the capital market and stock exchanges. Finally, the public sector was reorganized, as a prelude to privatization, into seventeen diversified and financially and managerially autonomous holding companies, severed from state financial support.

Beyond these urgently needed reforms, creating a macroeconomic environment supportive of private sector development implies a certain level of confidence in the sustainability of the government's reform policies and strategies. The announced government support to private sector initiative must be demonstrated in deeds. In that respect, the signals sent by the Egyptian government have been mixed. It has yet to demonstrate that the process of privatization, which is instrumental in realizing the shift in boundaries between the private and public sectors, is meaningful. Sending such a signal regarding privatization would entail moving a significant portion of public sector companies' assets to private ownership, which is yet to happen. The Egyptian government has to factually signal its complete commitment to private sector laissez faire.

The government's efforts to foster macroeconomic stability will bear fruit only if private sector operators are confident that the policies in place are sustainable. Aggregate demand-management policy (use of treasury bills, reduction of the state deficit, and so forth) have been successful in stabilization. However, how far is this policy sustainable? How soundly is the escalating domestic debt being managed? What are the features of the authorities' supply-side growth policy? All these and other questions remain to be answered and communicated clearly to the business community at large. Otherwise, private investment will continue to be too risky and hence too costly.

The regulatory environment

The government should shift its role from a market administrator using control tools such as approval and licensing of investment, to a registration agent that monitors and regulates the market through efficient standard-setting and deterring enforcement. It must be recognized that important steps have been undertaken toward that end. This is more so in the manufacturing sector where the main barriers to market entry to local and foreign private firms have been largely dismantled. Investment licensing approvals for manufacturing projects have become automatic; approval regulations for expansion, changes in product mix, and new products have been removed; and the process of streamlining overlapping regulatory jurisdictions between local governorates and central government authorities is underway.

Unfortunately, bureaucratic and regulatory obstacles to enterprises in other sectors are still severe. Businesses wishing to enter the market must go through three perplexing, time-consuming, and costly steps for final approval: investment activity licensing, legal incorporation, and establishment and operation licensing. Costs are further inflated by the requirement that new businesses pay 1.2 percent of their capital in stamp duty for registration. Companies wishing to obtain tax holiday and/or buy new land must also go through two additional stages. Investment incentives are very tightly administered and require cumbersome approval and monitoring procedures. In most cases land allocation is done administratively by the government which directs the businesses toward certain new industrial towns regardless of their locational economies. Furthermore, company incorporation can be done under different laws which entail different treatments regarding such important elements as supervisory authority, taxes, profit repatriation, and labor laws. Law 34 of 1976 also requires that all firms be registered in a commercial register which entails prior approval to operate by the local chamber of commerce.

Labor laws are equally restrictive to personnel management. Particularly detrimental are the employee disciplining and dismissal regulations. Disciplinary sanctions, which are set by governmental decrees, are not only nondeterrent but are very complex to administer. Dismissal is allowed only in case of company closure due to force majeure and is subject to approval by an interministerial committee. In effect, the law grants job security to even the most unproductive workers. Such a high level of protection is a strong disincentive to hire and train employees. International investors are usually scared away by the labor code's complexity and rigidity, perhaps the foremost constraint to entering the Egyptian market. Existing domestic private businesses manage to internalize the costs of dealing with labor regulations and thus gain a contestability-limiting advantage vis-à-vis potential foreign investors.

Rent control and tenant rights legislation, heavily biased in favor of tenants, acts as a strong disincentive to investment in the housing sector. Substantial amounts of savings are sunk in on-the-spot cash payments for housing either to own an apartment or to pay 'key money' for a rented one. The supply of housing units for lease is severely limited by the prohibitive rent control legislation. Rent control renders investment in housing unprofitable. Banks are very reluctant to finance housing projects, as housing units do not provide an adequate collateral in case of loan default. Evicting a tenant is virtually impossible and leads to long and costly court proceedings which end up, in the best of cases, only in forcing the tenant to pay a rent. Deregulation of rents may have the double positive effect of releasing savings toward private investment in productive assets and reactivating the housing construction sector.

Creating a predictable and contestable business environment in Egypt also implies the existence of two important legislative items which are currently either missing or weak: antitrust and property rights laws. There is currently no antitrust legislation, and property rights protection is weak. The provisions on novelty and exploitation rights are loosely defined and the penalties are nondeterrent. Such issues become crucial as the government proceeds with the privatization program. The lack of legislation that protects against adverse business practices is considered by businessmen and officials as a strong constraint on market deregulation and private sector development.

Government intervention

Egypt's economic and social development policies of the past two decades depended primarily on government intervention. Investment in large-scale projects in the public sector was expected to lead the economy to industrialization and was promoted by a combination of import substitution protection, subsidies, preferential credit terms, and priority access to foreign exchange. The government assumed the dominant role in investment in—and operation of—the educational system (from basic education to university and vocational training) and similarly in scientific research. The government also encouraged the private sector by targeting a host of incentives meant to attract new private local and international investment. It established state-run credit and other programs to promote private exports, extended subsidized credit to certain sectors, allocated low-price land in new industrial communities and free zones, and granted private producers protection from domestic and international competition, similar to that given to the public sector.

Government ownership of productive economic units as a tool of intervention seeking to profit from the previously mentioned 'catching up' effect may be strategically desirable in itself. However, the gains from such interventions erode when these units are loaded with other functions like redistribution of income or are used as instruments of implementation of the government's central plan. Enterprises, by definition, are not welfare agents. The blurring of boundaries between the role of the government-owned enterprises as agents of change and development and as instruments of redistribution of wealth seems to be the most controversial deviation that has occurred in the Egyptian economy.

The policy of guaranteeing lifetime employment in the public sector and of legislating high levels of job protection in the formal private sector has diminished the need for an effective social safety system. Today, social safety remains one that is largely based on informal social institutions and a strong sense of kinship among people. Unemployment benefits and pension payments are very low and their values have been eroded by inflation. The system's bureaucracy is also accused of being very inefficient, making the drawing of benefits an extremely tedious task. Perhaps the most serious deterrent to reforming labor laws in Egypt is the very low sense of security associated with the weaknesses of the social safety system.

Investment in research and development (R&D) in Egypt is performed by government research organizations and universities (also state controlled). Most of this research is of little use to either public or private enterprises. R&D in Egypt is accused of being too academic. Research centers and institutes are government bureaucracies insulated from market pressures. They are neither asked to bid for the funds they receive nor are they bound to be cost-effective or to return profits. Allocation of funds by the central government is not only insufficient, but it is done administratively with no attention to market needs. It is no surprise, therefore, that investment in R&D in Egypt is very low compared to other industrializing countries. During fiscal year 1992 R&D was worth 0.06 percent of Egypt's GDP, as compared to 0.2 percent in Turkey, 0.6 percent in Mexico, and 1.83 percent in Korea.

Similar problems are found in the education and health sectors. While the shares of these two sectors in government investment and recurrent expenditure have increased, the quality of their services has been steadily deteriorating. In education, the system suffers from low teachers' pay, inadequate instructional material, and inability to complete the implementation of improvements in the curricula. Technical training is of limited relevance to both public and private enterprises. At the heart of these problems are the weak civil service that runs the system, lack of cost recovery, and poor resource mobilization.

The main concern over state intervention has to do with its efficiency, and with the economic costs that come with it. For example, when the Egyptian government chose to promote the engineering industry over the past three decades, it went against the country's comparative advantage. Both private and public firms operating in this sector had to be heavily protected from competition. A quarter of a century later, a shift is observed in the comparative advantage of Egypt, and domestic resources costs (DRC) in the engineering subsector shows signs of being competitive within a free market. This appears to militate in favor of government intervention; but what were the costs to the economy of achieving this goal? And could it have been achieved more efficiently? Unfortunately, there are no estimates of these costs nor any analysis or debate of the policy options.

Evidence exists, however, as to how Egypt's interventionist approach at large resulted in loss of efficiency, financial imbalance, and loss of competitiveness among firms, and overall economic crisis. Among such evidence is the deterioration of the total factor productivity (TFP is the degree of efficiency with which inputs are used in the production process) for both public and private enterprises. TFP growth was in fact negative in 1992 and remained stagnant between 1982 and 1992. These losses could be explained partially by the distortions in the macroeconomic environment, and partially by the inability of interventionist institutions to substitute for market forces in allocating resources among participants, fostering the accumulation of human capital, and effecting technological advancement. Such institutions rely on concentrating information in the government bureaucracies which would presumably target and allocate resources—an impossible task. Information is simply very complex and fungible. Government institutions are not adept at generating the information that is needed to support investment decisions. This task should be left to the private sector.

There is no evidence that a continued government intervention could contribute to the hoped-for growth in the economy. The main thrust of the reform in the upcoming stage should be to divest the government from its central planning and interventionist public sector culture. Before the government makes any intervention, say to promote exports or develop small business, three conditions must be fulfilled. First, the civil service or public institutions that will be charged with making such interventions must be enabled by insulating them from political pressures, made more efficient, and held accountable for their performance. Second, the fault line between business administration and public administration must be clearly established; public enterprises must be considered as businesses first and should not have to fulfill other public interest roles. Enterprises should be granted sufficient autonomy to operate as enterprises, including flexible personnel and asset management. Third, intervention by the government should be brief and made only to complement the private sector, which should be given the leading role in investment and trade.

Existing government and private institutions

Efficient institutions of governance serve to reduce transaction costs with proper rule-setting, protection of rights, and efficient enforcement. A weak civil service and lack of coordination between the different branches and levels of government are perhaps the most serious obstacles to rule-setting and enforcement in Egypt. The decision-making process is always hampered by the scarcity of information, obsolete data management facilities, and poor working conditions. This is compounded by declining quality of skills of civil servants (the system cannot attract competent and dedicated staff with the low wages that it offers) and by the pronounced mismatch of skills and jobs (a result of the past policy of guaranteed public employment for graduates).

In the successful Far Eastern countries, civil service bureaucracies fulfilled the three most important principles for efficient administra-

Table 2-3
Comparison of annual wages in non-agricultural public and private employment (LE)

	Non-agricultural commodity sectors	Civil service & utilities	All non-agricultural sectors
1982–83			
Public	1,605	1,356	1,550
Private	1,132	–	1,086
1991–92			
Public			
Nominal	4,228	3,620	3,790
Real	862	738	773
Percentage real change	–46%	–45%	–50%
Private			
Nominal	5,193	–	4,583
Real	1,059	–	935
Percentage real change	–6.5%	–	–14%

Source: CAPMAS and Ministry of Planning

tion: merit-based recruitment and promotion, incentive-based compensation, and competitive career paths with attractive financial rewards for those who make it to the top. In Egypt, the civil service, although it might have such principles incorporated in its charters, did not adhere to them. Civil service careers have increasingly lost their appeal during the past decade. In 1982/83, average wages in the civil service, although lower than in the public enterprises, were superior to those of the private sector. Civil service pay did not, however, keep pace with inflation and declined in real terms by 45 percent between 1982 and 1992. Severe drops in real wages combined with the rigidity of the promotion system, excessive overstaffing (estimated to be over 40 percent), and the decline in the quality of education and training have all helped render the Egyptian bureaucracy unable to meet its public administration and governance functions.

Entrepreneurs are constantly in the position of dealing with line personnel who lack the understanding of the overall policy framework within which their own work occurs, who have no decision-making power, and who are more likely to delay and obstruct transactions than to expedite them. At best, they lack motivation to cooperate with proprietors to ensure that the provisions of the law are fulfilled. Rent-seeking and abuse of power are too often encountered by businessmen.

The judiciary and recourse institutions in Egypt fulfill their roles neither in the way of governing business transactions and protecting consumers or private property rights, nor in providing effective dispute resolution and contract enforcement mechanisms. Businesses need fast resolution of their disputes. Recent surveys show that 42 percent of private businesses had court cases that lasted two years or more and another 50 percent had outstanding disputes with officials.

The Egyptian judiciary must be brought up to par to deal with a growing volume of private transactions and attendant litigation. Legal experts advocate the improvement of arbitration institutions in Egypt as an alternative mechanism for providing more efficient dispute resolution. The need for such effective mechanisms, however, should not be limited to business–business litigation but should also provide recourses against government obstructions.

In every law that governs contracts and transactions between businesses, between a business and the government, or between a business and workers, a set of procedures and penalties is incorporated to allow for recourse against violators of its provisions. In Egypt, the recourse mechanisms are very weak and ineffective, and dramatically raise the cost of doing business. Two of the most relevant examples are the labor and tax administration laws. The recourse institutions in these two laws are biased in favor of labor or the tax authorities. The committees charged with acting as referees in case of disputes invariably have a majority government (or labor union) membership. Two-thirds to three-quarters of the members of the Tripartite Stoppage Committee (established in the labor law) and the Internal Appeals Committee (established by the tax law) come from either government or labor union backgrounds. If the disputes are not resolved by these committees, the cases are then taken to the judiciary. Extended periods of committee deliberation and negotiation force most proprietors to unproductively dedicate up to 30 percent of their time to problem solving with government bureaucracy. Most businesses prefer to try to negotiate with officials informally through personal contacts rather than use formal channels.

Private business associations can serve as an important institutional relay between the government and the private sector. In Egypt, such associations include the Federation of Egyptian Chambers of Commerce, the Egyptian Federation of Industrial Chambers, a limited number of independently chartered associations, and a few organizations chartered under protocols with foreign governments. Most of these associations suffer from stifling regulations and laws that undermine their capacity to represent the interests of private businesses.

The Egyptian Chambers of Commerce are under the supervision of the Ministry of Supply and Domestic Trade. There is a total of twenty-five chambers covering all the country's governorates except South Sinai. Membership is mandatory for all proprietors and totals an estimated three million. Half the Chambers' board of directors is elected by the members and the other half is appointed by the parent ministry. Delegated authorities are narrowly defined and subject to be overridden by the ministry.

The Egyptian Federation of Industrial Chambers was established in 1928 and organized by industry groups since 1937. Membership is compulsory for all enterprises (public and private) with a capital over LE5,000 or employing twenty-five workers or more. There are currently thirteen industrial chambers with an estimated thirteen thousand members. The role of the chambers in representing the interests of their members is constrained by state intervention. One-third of the federation's board of directors is appointed by the Ministry of Industry and two-thirds by the General Assembly. The role of the federation is tightly controlled by the right of the ministry to dismiss the board of directors; the obligation to send the board's composition to the ministry for endorsement; and the presence at every board meeting of a representative of the Industrial Monitoring Authority.

A number of businessmen's associations like the Egyptian Businessmen's Association and the Alexandrian Businessmen's Association have been created under Law 32 of 1964 which governs the establishment of any association of private citizens. According to this law, all associations must be registered with the Ministry of Social Affairs, which can exert extensive control. Up to half of the members of a board of directors can be appointed by the ministry. The ministry may also place items on the agenda of a board's meeting; it can remove names from the list of nominees to the board and can nullify elections; and it can also dissolve general assemblies for a variety of reasons including incompetence and violation of the law. Associations are also severely restricted in their ability to raise funds, as they must apply for a license from the Administration of Social Affairs at the governorate level.

No two associations, say for representing business interests, are allowed to establish in the same city or governorate. Articles 3 and 12 of Law 32 of 1964 both grant the Ministry of Social Affairs the undisputed right to deny registration for an association that is judged as "not being needed by the society." Not surprisingly, the leadership of these associations must rely on their contacts at the highest levels of government to fend off unnecessary bureaucratic obstruction to their roles as representatives of private sector interests.

A VISION FOR CHANGE

The development recipe that Egypt needs to adopt is very similar to that of the successful Far Eastern countries: a surge in private domestic investment, a rigorous improvement of its human capital, and a rapid move toward international competitiveness. Its development strategy, however, must differ insofar as it must take into account the differences in economic, institutional, and cultural conditions. Add to that the change in the world's economic environment since the 1960s and the 1970s, when the Far Eastern countries were on their path to development.

The government will need to attend to strengthening its governance institutions; restructuring the education, health, and other public services sectors; and rebuilding the social safety system; all tasks that will most certainly tax its capacity. The Egyptian private sector on the other hand is still young, relatively small, and will also need to undergo structural changes while it takes on the investment, employment, export, and growth challenges that the country's economy faces. Shifting the boundaries to expand private sector participation in Egypt is not enough. In fact, it is not feasible if it is not done concurrently with an environment that forces efficiency in the private sector, the civil service, and other public institutions such as the judiciary. The key feature of the reforms in the upcoming stage should be the setting up of an environment that heightens contestability for all operators in the market, state and private alike.

The strategy for change must be based on a private–public partnership. It is merely stating a fact to say that, so far, the private sector has not been sufficiently involved in, nor properly informed of, the management of the Egyptian economy. The new rules of the game must be formulated jointly without losing sight of free competition and fair play. New channels for communication with the private sector must be established. This could be achieved by enabling private business groups and associations, by encouraging them to diversify and compete over interest representation, and by formalizing an all-inclusive public–private forum of debate on economic management.

AGENDA FOR REFORM

The following is the reform agenda put forward by Egypt's private sector. Given the need for further in-depth analysis, the following items have not been prioritized (this task is best left to joint private–

public task forces, where the chances of informed prioritization are greater).

Reforming the legal and regulatory environment

1. Remove all barriers to entry, operation, and exit of private businesses in all sectors of the economy, whether in company formation, activity licensing, E&O licensing, land acquisition, employment, taxation, or liquidation and bankruptcy.
2. Remove price controls on private-sector-delivered health and education services and allow for diversification and differentiation of these services.
3. Modernize commercial laws to respond to modern developments in business and financial transactions, especially in the finance sector.
4. Reform housing rent control laws to make them more equitable for both owners and tenants, in a way that improves the return on investment and reduces the risk of lending in this sector.
5. Introduce antitrust and fair-play laws that regulate investment and operations of public or private enterprises.

Strengthening public and private institutions

6. Introduce a temporary system or a sunset law (until the civil service and the judiciary reforms are completed) that allows fast and effective recourse by private enterprises against malpractice by government administrations (like tax offices, municipalities, social insurance offices, labor offices, etc.).
7. Reform the social security system to bring it up to a standard that would sustain higher mobility of labor and allow for a more efficient domestic labor market.
8. Adopt a policy of ex post selective inspections and punishment for regulatory violations, instead of the current ex ante enforcement method; prevent the practice of issuing or enforcing laws with a retroactive effect.
9. Accelerate the civil service reform program with special attention to better compensation and training, in particular in agencies involved in business–business and government–business transactions.
10. Completely overhaul the tax administration policies and procedures; abolish the system of full inspection of all taxpayers' accounts; and upgrade Egypt's accounting standards to be in line with internationally accepted ones.

11. Reform the judicial system by allowing more competitive employment and personnel policies and by revising litigation procedures and rules to reduce incentives for case delays.
12. Liberalize the formation and operation of business associations to enable them to diversify and compete over interest representation and advocate their members' rights.
13. Remove restrictions on private sector market research and foster the dissemination of economic and legal information; encourage the participation of private for-profit firms that could provide such services.

Shifting the boundaries of private sector participation

14. Accelerate the privatization of state-owned enterprises through sales, management contracts, lease with option to buy, or other forms.
15. Expand the scope of Egypt's privatization program to include sectors such as telecommunications, electricity, transport, media, health, education, etc.
16. Break down public enterprises' and public authorities' monopolies and/or oligopolies in sectors that are not natural monopolies, such as all manufacturing subsectors, transportation, port handling and services, banking, electricity generation, water treatment, telecommunications, insurance, etc.

Three

Private Sector Development: Realizing the New Paradigm for Growth in the Middle East

Caio Koch-Weser

This is a time of great hope for renewed and peaceful progress in the Middle East and North Africa. The years 1993 and 1994 were for this region the equivalent of 1989 and 1990 for the countries of Eastern Europe and the former Soviet Union. Developments considered almost unimaginable only two years ago have combined to lay the foundations for a new geopolitical order in the region—one that offers unprecedented opportunities for building a better tomorrow for all of its peoples. And of course, Egypt has played a leading role, starting with the historic breakthrough of the Camp David accords, in building a comprehensive and enduring peace.

But the unfolding peace process cannot by itself guarantee the economic development needed to bring about substantial and long overdue improvements in the living conditions of ordinary people. Geopolitical stability alone cannot restore growth. This brings us to the central theme that will be explored here. How can the countries of the region best meet the economic and social challenge of creating broad-based prosperity as well as peace? In addressing this theme, the discussion will follow three broad topics: first, some of the economic challenges facing the region; second, the core components of a new private-sector-oriented strategy for sustainable and shared economic growth; and third, Egypt's progress to date in adopting this strategy, and some key areas for future action.

ECONOMIC CHALLENGES

In principle, many of the preconditions for a leap forward into prosperity already exist in the region. These include a potentially large regional market of over 200 million people; a favorable geographical location for profitable international trade and successful integration into global markets; an increasingly educated population with a long history of entrepreneurship; a shared heritage of strong spiritual, cultural, and social values; rich endowment with one of the world's most prized commodities, oil; investment resources—currently held overseas but potentially available for development—running into the hundreds of billions of dollars; and world-renowned attractions for international tourism.

These conditions favorable to dynamic economic expansion are increasingly being matched by a regionwide consensus that a new paradigm for development, based on outward-looking, competitive, and private-sector-led strategies for growth, must be the central ingredient for meeting the social and economic needs of the peoples of the region. The advent of peace will make it possible to unleash the energies of governments and peoples so that they may realize this paradigm, enter into a race for prosperity rather than for armaments, and substitute shared growth for shared perceptions of external threats as a basis for social cohesion. But the region also faces formidable challenges. The following are just four such challenges.

First, long-term growth in average income per head of population has been inadequate. Only a generation ago, the developing economies of the Maghreb and the Mashreq had an average per capita income roughly equal to that of the East Asian developing countries. Today, superior economic performance and rapid reductions in population growth rates in East Asia have created a surge in incomes that has left the Middle East and North Africa (MENA) region far behind, to the point where income per head in this set of MENA countries is less than half that of the East Asian group. If MENA countries had had average East Asian rates of growth, Egypt would now have a per capita income substantially above Colombia's, and Jordan's income per head would be higher than Brazil's.

Second, the combination of slow economic growth and rapid population growth has helped to produce unacceptably high levels of unemployment and poverty in many MENA countries. These twin evils are economically undesirable, humanly degrading, and socially disruptive. And the fruits of such growth as has occurred have not been shared by all segments of society. Income inequality has actually increased in some countries as overall standards of living have declined. Alleviating poverty and inequality will require not only massive new employment generation; the fact that the majority of the poor are currently working suggests that not just more, but more productive, higher quality (and therefore better paid) jobs are needed.

Third, the MENA region also still has far to go in terms of basic indicators of social well-being. For example, life expectancy at birth is one of the most fundamental measures of human health. Although average life expectancy has risen substantially, from fifty-six years in 1975 to sixty-four years by the early 1990s, this latter figure is barely higher than the average for South Asia, even though the MENA region's per capita income is far greater. Literacy, the ability to read and write, is a fundamental measure of educational attainment and is critical for both individual achievement and national economic growth. Although MENA countries as a group spend a far higher proportion of their national income on education than any other developing region of the world, only a little over half of the MENA region's population aged fifteen and over is literate, barely above the average for sub-Saharan Africa.

Finally, and underlying all other challenges facing the region, investment, the basic fuel for growth, has been both low and inefficient in most MENA countries. In recent years, the level of investment has hovered around 20 percent of national income, far below the 25 percent or more needed to ensure that income growth does much more than keep up with population growth. Part of the problem has been the macroeconomic and political uncertainty that has caused massive capital flight; an estimated total of about $180 billion was held overseas by MENA investors in 1991. This is money that might have been used to build new industries and create more jobs and more wealth in MENA countries. Meanwhile, private investment flows in the opposite direction, into MENA countries from abroad, have been very limited. The combined total of foreign direct investment in the non-oil economies of the region was barely $1.3 billion in 1992, compared to nearly $1.8 billion in Indonesia alone. Still more importantly, investment has been inefficient; consider the following two illustrations of the situation.

First, and as mentioned above, literacy is low in MENA countries despite high rates of investment in education. This paradox reflects a socially and economically inefficient pattern of educational investment. MENA countries have devoted too little to primary schooling—only about one-fifth of total funding compared to over one-third in East Asia, for example—in comparison to higher levels of education. The result is a combination of pervasive illiteracy and an army of unemployed graduates—a combination that retards growth and contributes to social alienation and unrest.

Second, and more generally, domestic investment, and production as a whole, has been skewed in favor of the public sector at the expense of the private sector. State-owned enterprises have dominated not only the provision of basic services such as water, electricity, and telecommunications, but also productive sectors such as manufacturing. These enterprises have in many cases been subject to little or no commercial discipline; they have also often been expected to meet government social objectives rather than being allowed to operate economically. As a result, the massive investment they have absorbed has frequently ended up creating debt rather than wealth. Additionally, they have not been able to effectively meet national socio-economic goals, such as employment promotion. State-owned enterprises in MENA countries have created less than half the jobs per unit of investment that private firms have; the disparity is even more striking in manufacturing, where the private sector typically creates nearly five times as many jobs per unit of investment as state firms.

THE WAY AHEAD: THE PARADIGM OF PRIVATE-SECTOR–LED GROWTH

The challenges described are real and substantial, but they can be overcome. The new paradigm for development mentioned above is based on using a liberated, competitive private sector as the engine of growth. This new paradigm has worked and is continuing to work outstandingly well in other parts of the developing world. East Asia is the example most often quoted, but there are plenty of examples of success from other regions, notably including the reforming economies of Latin America and Eastern Europe. What are some of the characteristics of these successful economies?

First, they have what economists call the 'policy fundamentals' right. They have established a stable macroeconomic environment by holding down budget deficits and keeping external debt at manageable levels. Equally importantly, they have promoted both domestic and international competitiveness by pursuing increasingly outward-looking trade and economic policies. They have reduced and eliminated tariffs and subsidies. Rather than penalizing exports, they have encouraged them; and where they have provided direct support to domestic industries, this support has been limited in duration. It has also been performance based, often involving creating competitive contests among firms rather than providing shelters for inefficiency.

Second, the countries that have successfully implemented the new paradigm of private-sector-led growth have evolved a philosophy of governance under which the appropriate role of the state has been to support and facilitate, rather than to manage or directly participate in, the productive sectors of the economy. As part of their supportive role, these governments have put in place a business-friendly operating environment. They have reformed and simplified regulatory and administrative systems, so as to make it easier for firms to set up business and to grow. They have designed legal systems that have guaranteed property rights (including intellectual property rights), eased entry into (and if necessary exit from) productive sectors, and provided workers with essential protection against exploitation without carrying protection so far that it limits labor mobility. They have established fiscal systems and financial sectors that have encouraged private savings and investment. And they have fostered competent and honest civil services and judiciaries.

Third, these governments have played an active role where their intervention could make a positive difference. They have invested efficiently in the high quality human capital and supportive infrastructure that firms need if they are to prosper in an increasingly integrated and skills-oriented global economy. They have also supported technological development and product quality upgrading. They have promoted technology transfer from abroad by liberalizing licensing requirements and eliminating controls on foreign direct investment. They have encouraged indigenous technological development through well-designed support for applied research and development. And they have established local standards institutions to help bring the quality of output up to international levels.

Fourth, most of these countries have worked to ensure that the benefits of growth have been shared among all segments of society. They have operated on the basis of a covenant with their peoples, sometimes explicitly and effectively articulated in an inclusive and broadly appealing vision that the national wealth will be used to improve the lives of all citizens. They have put in place social safety nets, education and health care systems, municipal services, and housing programs that have helped to address the needs of the poor. And they have promoted capitalism with a human face, curbing the exploitative excesses of the past and emphasizing investment designed to create more and better quality private sector jobs. The resulting expansion of incomes and purchasing power has in turn stimulated more investment; this virtuous spiral has created rapid long-run growth accompanied by reductions in inequality. As a result of this shared growth, they have developed relatively cohesive societies that have weathered economic bad times together as well as sharing the benefits from good ones.

There is no reason why MENA countries should not be able to adopt the new paradigm whose features have just been outlined. Before turning to Egypt's experience in moving toward it, let us quickly summarize some of the steps taken by the World Bank's other active partners in the region toward laying the foundations for private-sector-led and broadly shared growth.

Most of these countries, including Algeria, Morocco, Tunisia, Jordan, and Iran, have either completed or are well advanced with programs of macroeconomic stabilization. Morocco and Tunisia in particular have moved well beyond this point. Since the late 1980s, Morocco has taken major steps to improve competitiveness by increasingly deregulating markets of all kinds, abolishing monopolies, and privatizing state-owned enterprises. It has improved the operating environment for Moroccan exporters and producers for the domestic market, and for foreign investors, by easing institutional and regulatory constraints, including abolition of controls on foreign ownership and repatriation of profits. Over the same period, Tunisia has liberalized import restrictions, price controls, investment and credit authorizations, regulations on repatriation of dividends by foreign investors, and most interest rates. Both countries have not only liberalized their trade regimes but are also taking steps toward greater integration with European Community markets. Beginning in 1989, Jordan has undertaken a substantial and ongoing program of trade liberalization. In addition to continuing this effort, the government is considering reforms in the financial and banking sector, along with commercialization and privatization of public enterprises. Algeria has begun to liberalize prices and tariffs, along with the legal and institutional framework within which businesses operate. It is also beginning the difficult process of public enterprise reform, and has been a regional innovator in social safety net reform based on a new program of targeted cash transfers to the poor. Both Iran and Lebanon face special problems of massive reconstruction, but both have moved toward stabilizing their economies, and Lebanon in particular, along with the West Bank and Gaza, has committed itself to a strategy of private-sector-led recovery and growth. Finally, Yemen also faces severe short-term difficulties, but had begun to consider a comprehensive stabilization effort before the recent political upheavals.

REALIZING THE PARADIGM: EGYPT'S PROGRESS AND PRIORITIES

The following is a brief assessment of where Egypt stands in its efforts to realize the new paradigm of private-sector-led growth. Egypt has always had a unique position of leadership in the region. Its rich historical, cultural, and intellectual identity is measured in millennia, not in centuries or decades. In modern times it has played a substantial political role on the world stage as well as regionally. In economic terms, too, Egypt carries tremendous weight in the region. It accounts for over 20 percent of the total population of the Middle East and North Africa. If countries mainly dependent on oil are excluded, it has the region's largest economy.

But Egypt also has the region's lowest per capita income after Yemen's, and a third of its population lives in deep poverty. Moreover, recent governments have had to contend with the legacy of the centralized command economy of the 1950s and 1960s. By the beginning of the present decade, the public sector still absorbed more than half of all investment and accounted for nearly three-quarters of manufacturing output. Both public and private enterprises operated within an economic environment featuring distorted prices, heavy protection from import competition, massive subsidies, increasingly unmanageable budget deficits, and crippling external debt.

The new direction the government has taken since 1991 is notable in that its central vision has involved abandoning the old command economy paradigm, turning instead to a market-friendly development strategy—one in which a dynamic, competitive private sector will be liberated to play the leading role in restoring growth, creating new productive employment, and thereby helping to reduce poverty. The first order of business has been macroeconomic stabilization. The spending cuts and price increases undertaken for this purpose have paid off, with sharp reductions in the budget deficit and inflation. The government has also taken difficult but critical steps to increase competitiveness, through a combination of trade and price liberalization, subsidy reduction, and commitment to an ambitious program of privatizing state-owned enterprises in the productive sectors. It has also implemented a substantial financial liberalization package and has begun to dismantle some of the most onerous components of the regulatory regime.

These are important achievements, but they are only the beginning. The macroeconomic outlook remains fragile in several major respects. The economy is still vulnerable to external shocks, and there is a danger that the previous external debt service problem may be translated into an equally crippling domestic debt service problem. Meanwhile, the hard fact is that the private-sector-oriented structural reforms undertaken to date have not yet brought forth a supply response from private investors. Why is this? Part of the reason is continuing business uncertainty about the economic climate, which in turn reflects the fact that the reform agenda still has far to go, and its practical impact has thus far been relatively limited. To address these problems, the reform effort needs to be pressed forward with new vigor, and its rhetoric needs to be matched by urgent action on a broad front designed to bring speedy and concrete results. The second phase of the government's Economic Reform and Structural Adjustment Program (ERSAP), which is intended to deepen and accelerate the reform process, is therefore welcomed. Below are three core objectives to be served by this process, and some of the specific policy actions included in the government's program that will help realize them.

The first and absolutely fundamental objective must be to build business confidence in the depth and durability of reform. Firms will be willing to invest only when they can be confident that the economic environment is going to remain favorable to private-sector-led growth. This means continuing to maintain a sound and stable macroeconomic framework. And within this framework, it means taking further steps toward financial sector and legal and regulatory reform. With respect to the financial sector, banks need to be encouraged to offer firms longer term credit than they can currently obtain, funding needs to be made available to the currently poorly served small business sector, and Egypt's capital markets need to be developed as reliable sources of equity financing for new and expanding enterprises. Legal and regulatory systems need to provide business people with an operating environment that offers timely and dependable justice, secures property rights and contracts, and makes it easier for firms, including small businesses, to incorporate, invest, produce, expand, and profit. Top priority must go to rapid acceleration of the pace and scope of the government's program for privatization of state-owned enterprises. Perhaps no other single aspect of the reform process is a better touchstone of the government's commitment to changing the whole system of economic management and governance in favor of the private sector.

A second and equally important objective must be to continue the process of building competitiveness. This involves action on a number of fronts. It includes developing skills, upgrading product quality, and removing bureaucratic barriers to efficiency. It also includes additional tariff reductions and new initiatives to eliminate subsidies and monopolies. Some of these measures may not be wholly welcome to the business community in the short term. But firms, and national economies, cannot prosper in today's increasingly competitive world unless their costs and prices are at or near international levels. One way of easing the transition and reducing the uncertainties involved in implementing the next stages of Egypt's competition policy would be to establish genuinely effective consultative mechanisms between business and government—for example, the joint business–government councils pioneered in a number of East Asian countries and now being adopted in Morocco. Of course, arrangements of this kind would also contribute to building and maintaining business confidence.

Third, but emphatically not least, it will be essential to pursue the objective of ensuring that the fruits of growth are shared among all segments of society. Here some of the priority actions involved are directly within the government's control. They include moving toward universal provision of basic education and health services for all citizens, reforming the social security system, and designing a social safety net for the poor that will provide enhanced and better-targeted benefits to those most in need. But ultimately, achieving sustainable and shared growth will depend on improving both the quantity and quality of job opportunities in the economy, which brings us back to the primacy of economic reform, and its fruits in the shape of a dynamic, investment-and-employment-oriented private sector.

CONCLUSION

This is a time of unprecedented potential for peace and prosperity in the MENA region. It is also a moment of enormous opportunity for Egypt to match its leadership in the pursuit of peace with decisive action on the economic front. It is understood that Egypt's reform agenda is massive, but realizing it will have tremendous payoffs. If it is pursued with vigor and determination, it could form the basis for nothing less than an 'Egyptian economic miracle' based on rapid and sustainable economic growth led by a liberated and invigorated private sector.

Bringing about this outcome will not be easy. It will require profound changes in entrenched habits of thought and behavior. It will also require sustained and simultaneous action in all the areas outlined above. They are all interdependent, and working on them piecemeal will reduce if not preclude the chances of obtaining their maximum benefits.

Even more importantly, just as action needs to be concerted, so the actors involved need to work in concert with one another. We must therefore call for a combined effort on the part of all concerned parties to support private-sector-led growth. With respect to the role of the World Bank group, it will help in whatever way it can, working in close collaboration with both the government and the private sector. It would hope to support all aspects of Egypt's reform program with technical assistance and advice—based on worldwide experience with best practices of other reforming economies—providing financing where appropriate and subject to the government's priorities, including support for the private sector and for the effective public services that help make private sector development possible. And support is not confined to the work of the World Bank itself. It would also expect the work of its affiliates, the International Finance Corporation (IFC) and the Multinational Investment Guarantee Agency (MIGA), to contribute increasingly to the flow of private sector investment into Egypt's economy. Egypt is a member of MIGA, which provides foreign investors with guarantees against noncommercial risk and offers investment promotion services for member countries. The IFC has a substantial investment portfolio in Egypt, amounting to $140 million in nineteen separate enterprises. This represents nearly one-third of total IFC investment in the MENA region, and is IFC's second largest MENA country portfolio.

But successful reform and the prosperity it brings will ultimately depend far less on external support than on tapping the joint energies of the business community, the government, the intelligentsia, and above all, the people of Egypt as a whole. Sustained public–private sector cooperation will ensure that Egypt realizes the vision so long sought by its leaders and its people—a vision of a society that is both dynamic and just, a society in which the aspirations of all Egypt's people can be fulfilled and in which the well-being of all her citizens is finally assured.

Four

Legal and Regulatory Framework for Private Sector Development in Egypt

Ibrahim Shihata

INTRODUCTION

A clearer understanding is needed to appreciate how the private sector can be a major engine of growth which is both equitable and sustainable. The role of an appropriate legal and regulatory framework is key to this understanding. The importance of an appropriate legal framework, including an effective judiciary, cannot be overstated for a market system that works efficiently. Market mechanisms require competition in a level playing field and assume a great measure of certainty and predictability in the applicable rules. Without an appropriate and properly enforced legal framework, such market mechanisms will inevitably be replaced by personal relationships and corrupting practices. Without actual legal protection, those who do not have influence or money, especially the weakest and disadvantaged segments of society, are bound to suffer as 'crony capitalism' creeps in, leading at best to the enrichment of a few. It is important to note that practically all observers and researchers recognize the necessity of legal and judicial reform, and one describes the predicament of the judiciary as "the strongest constraint on business transactions" to private sector development in Egypt today.

We must realize at the outset that an appropriate legal framework does not consist only of 'good' rules. Equally essential are the processes through which these rules are made and applied, and the institutions in charge of their application and enforcement. If the processes are arbitrary or unduly complex, or if the institutions are poorly staffed, ineffective, or dishonest, not even the best rules in the books will be of much help. The situation is much worse, of course, if inefficient institutions following arbitrary and complex processes apply rules which are unfair and/or unjustified. Clearly, a situation like this cannot allow any system to be sustained, let alone to compete in the world markets.

A legal and regulatory system, with its rules, processes, and institutions, that serves the purposes of economic development and allows the private sector to grow must not only ensure competition and allow prices and wages to be determined rationally; it must also protect property rights and contract enforcement. Contrary to what many people believe, such protection is essential for the growth of small business in particular. The protection of property and the enforcement of contracts enable individuals with a little property and without political connections or influence to make investments. They promote the accumulation of physical and human capital. They lower transaction costs. They help generate a better distribution of income and wealth. And above all, they give investors and consumers alike a sense of security and confidence in the system that is badly needed, especially for the commitment of long-term capital.

In this context, legislative policy is intertwined with economic and social policies. Through legislative and regulatory action, economic and social policies are translated into rules and procedures, the effective application of which enables societies to achieve their objectives. Experience shows that successful legislative policies are those which are based on the presumption of permissibility, that is, those which assume that prohibitions, limitations, and approvals are the exception rather than the general rule. Interestingly, this presumption is one of the basic principles of Islamic jurisprudence *(usul al-fiqh)* which recognizes permissibility as the general rule. This principle seems nonetheless to be commonly ignored in many countries proclaiming Islamic law as the source of legislation.

Allowing economic agents to work with a minimum degree of state intervention has long been advocated in the Arab culture, most notably by the fifteenth-century writings of Ibn Khaldun. Egypt did not need to learn this from the World Bank. This is not only good economics; it is also good law. Furthermore, it respects human dignity; it assumes goodness in people and relies more on ex post enforceable sanctions in case of violation of established rules than on the prior approval of every possible act. By keeping the limits to the minimum dictated by the exigencies of public interest, the state also ensures the effectiveness of the limits it introduces. Such effectiveness is often lost in systems based on the presumption of prohibition and burdened with excessive constraints. Drawing the right boundaries between state and market forces is one of the fundamentals of successful legislative policies; it is also the underlying issue in any discussion on private sector development.

The general remarks above are a prelude to some more specific comments on the legal framework in Egypt. The discussion below starts with some general sources of uncertainty in the Egyptian legal system which need to be addressed; it then briefly touches on some areas of legal and judicial reform which require particular attention in light of comparative experience, including reforms which have not been mentioned elsewhere.

MAIN SOURCES OF UNCERTAINTY IN THE LEGAL SYSTEM

Certainty and predictability are no doubt hallmarks of a legal environment conducive to private sector development. Yet, three areas of concern shed doubts on Egypt's legal environment. First is the excessive use of legislation and regulation and the frequency of the changes they undergo. It is difficult, even for the government employees in charge, to know all the applicable rules regulating a certain activity. In spite of considerable liberalization in recent years, many approvals are still, for no convincing purpose, required before initiating many economic activities, and too many 'fees' are attached to these approvals. Numerous limitations were introduced to achieve short-term social objectives or political gains without consideration of their long-term impact, including their negative impact in the long run on the very objectives they were meant to serve (e.g., arbitrary rent control, excessive tax rates, rigid employment conditions). Past abuses resulting from the absence of any regulations in certain areas often led to excessive state intervention (e.g., the legislative provisions responding to the scandal of the so-called 'Islamic money management companies'). The pressing needs of special circumstances, the special interests of powerful groups, and the prolonged state of war or emergency have in the past added further restrictions to an already heavily regulated system. The result is a mosaic of a tremendous number of laws and regulations, some dating to the time of the Ottomans, which stifle competition, impede innovation, and invite corruption. In their totality, they give conflicting signals, increase business costs, and require constant changes at the expense of certainty. Worse still, they have led to the establishment of a formidable hidden economy with informal and sometimes illicit sectors. Comparative experience shows that prior rigorous analysis and adequate consultation are the best guarantee for the making of rules which are fair and durable. Crisis situations should not lead to the adoption of legislation which outlives the crisis and continues to impose constraints no longer justified after the disappearance of the crisis. The work that has started in Egypt to purify the legal and regulatory framework from its intricate net of limitations, approvals, and meaningless signatures still has a long way to go.

This is not to suggest that regulation is not necessary. On the contrary, competition is not an alternative to regulation; it should be its direct beneficiary. What matters in the end is to have an effective legal and regulatory regime which serves clear economic and social purposes on a sustained basis—a regime which avoids arbitrariness and excesses, promotes and maintains competition, and prevents market concentration and the abuse of a dominant market position by a single operator. Once this regime is established, it should not be subjected to frequent changes.

The second source of uncertainty is the growing gap between constitutional principles and new legislation and regulations. This point has been referred to in a number of papers; unfortunately, it is true. The present constitution of Egypt is clearly based on a different ideology from that which underlies recent laws and regulations. It explicitly provides for comprehensive central planning and endows the state with pervasive powers in the economic sphere. It makes the public sector the backbone of the economy, describing it as "the vanguard of progress in all spheres." This is hardly consistent with the new trend toward privatization and a market economy. Pro-market laws and a socialist constitution cannot coexist for a long time. Their coexistence is bound to create confusion and hesitation on the part of long-term investors. They can also add greatly to the cost of their investments.

The third and last source of uncertainty that must be mentioned is the constant claim of inconsistency between the present legal system and the principles of sharia. Under Article 2 of the present constitution, as amended in 1980, "the principles of Islamic Sharia are the source of legislation." Yet claims abound to the effect that many existing laws are inconsistent with the sharia. This is not necessarily correct, at least as far as civil and commercial law are concerned; but since this is a controversial matter, it is bound to generate continuous uncertainty until it is decisively settled. Unfortunately, the Constitutional Court's ruling in the 1985 decision regarding the constitutionality of Article 226 of the Civil Code (which provides for interest on delayed due payments) was not helpful in this respect, as it left the matter open for all practical purposes. The point here is not to argue for or against the application of the sharia, especially as the present civil and commercial codes are not necessarily inconsistent with the sharia. The point is that there is a dire need to eliminate doubt and to have a system which provides a clear and stable basis for the conduct of economic activities and commercial transactions.

SPECIFIC AREAS OF LEGAL AND JUDICIAL REFORM

While the Civil Code of 1949 remains a solid basis for the legal system, the much older commercial code and the various laws and regulations on companies, labor, taxation, investment, land tenure and registration, civil procedure, as well as those organizing the judiciary, require basic reforms. Many countries which undertook comprehensive legal reforms benefited from establishing a central unit in charge of this task. Such a unit acted as an internal coordinator of the legal reform process and of the external technical and financial assistance available for this purpose. Quite often, the unit was attached to the office of the prime minister or the head of state. Whether coordinated through such a unit or not, successful legal reform involved the local legal communities in the countries concerned and was accompanied by extensive programs of information, education, and training. The remarks below are confined to a few selected areas of needed legal reform, mentioning as appropriate, in telegraphic language, examples of what has been done in countries facing similar problems.

The judiciary

Problems facing the judiciary in developing countries are typically of four types: 1) problems resulting from the lack of independence and the interference by the executive branch of government; 2) physical problems related to the shortage of buildings, facilities, supplies, and financial resources; 3) human resources problems related to the number and quality of the judges and other court officers, their training and work methods as well as their salaries and benefits; and 4) problems related to the judicial process, including the system of case management and the applicable procedures. While the independence of the judiciary is reasonably established in Egypt, the system clearly suffers from the three other categories of problems. Mentioned below are a few reforms which have been particularly helpful in reducing the backlog of cases in other countries.

The creation of specialized banking courts in Pakistan and India helped greatly in expediting the recovery of bank debts and encouraged banks to expand lending to small businesses. The reform included the establishment of a large number of these courts. Each court consists of a single judge who has the power to deliver judgment and order execution except in a limited number of cases involving very large amounts where appeal is permissible. Specialized bankruptcy courts, established in other countries like the U.S., with the power to impose financial plans for the restructuring of enterprises have helped not only in the speedy resolution of disputes but also in avoiding liquidation in most cases.

Referral of small claims and petty offenses to lay judges (designated dignitaries) has greatly helped in restricting the number of cases submitted to courts of law in countries like the U.S., Peru, and Singapore. In practice, many of these cases are settled by agreement of the parties under the guidance of the lay judge, and few of the decisions are appealed.

Adoption of rigorous case management systems have been particularly helpful in state courts in the U.S. as well as in Singapore. Examples include pretrial conferences to determine the status of cases and the preparedness of the parties. The early screening of cases through initiating judges is followed by the adoption of fixed dates, the refusal of adjournment as a general rule, and the restriction of appeals. The system of case flow management is subject to a strict regime of information and monitoring by executive judges, each with administrative responsibility for a cluster of courtrooms.

The establishment of commercial arbitration centers in many countries has been particularly helpful in deciding commercial and investment disputes. Egypt now has the Afro–Asian Cairo Arbitration Center. This could be complemented by local centers not only for arbitration but also for conciliation (80 percent of cases in Colombia are now being settled through conciliation centers) and for mediation. Mediation has roots in Islamic jurisprudence and is provided for in certain cases under existing proceedings in Egypt. The scope for expansion in this and similar systems (like the American system of 'early neutral evaluation') is great.

The use of computers and other office technology systems in the assignment of cases to different courts and in the reproduction of court transcripts has greatly helped in saving time and in avoiding typical problems of unequal workloads and the filing of cases with the wrong courts in countries like Argentina and Jamaica.

Tax law

In spite of several improvements in recent years both in tax legislation and administration and of impressive increases in revenues, the tax regime in Egypt still suffers from many shortcomings. Too many taxes, with excessive rates on high brackets of income and excessive exemptions, characterize the legislation. Delayed auditing of all taxpayers and cumbersome dispute settlement procedures characterize tax administration. Clearly, there is a need for further improvements especially by reducing stamp taxes, the rates of certain direct taxes, and the exemptions therefrom. In Mexico, where the previous tax regime had similar shortcomings, recent reforms made a big difference both on business incentives and tax revenues. A speech by the then Mexican finance minister during the 1994 IMF–World Bank Joint Annual Meeting in Madrid included some particularly relevant remarks:

> The main elements of the tax reform were the reduction in the number of taxes and in tax rates, the widening of the taxpayer base and the strict enforcement of fiscal laws in order to fight fiscal evasion. In 1988 there were nineteen federal taxes, today there are less than half. The corporate income tax rate was reduced from 39.2 percent in 1988 to 34 percent since 1993 . . . the value added tax rate . . . has been reduced from a dual rate of 20 percent and 15 percent to a single one of 10 percent. The maximum rate for the personal income tax was reduced from 50 percent to 35 percent. Workers on the lower end of the income tax schedule receive an income tax credit which implies a positive transfer from the government. For workers that receive one minimum wage, the income tax credit implies an increase of 13 percent in their disposable income. [These changes] constitute the easy part of the tax reform: less taxes and lower rates. The difficult part . . . consists of increasing the number of taxpayers and rigorously enforcing the tax law. Excluding salaried workers whose taxes are withheld in their workplaces, the taxpayer base increased from 1.7 million taxpayers in 1988 to 5.5 million in 1993 . . . more than five hundred cases [of tax evasion] have been presented. As a result, notwithstanding the reduction in tax rates, tax revenues have increased 35 percent in real terms, while GDP has increased by 18.8 percent in the same period.

The lesson is clear. Similar lessons could be drawn from the earlier actions taken by Chile which had demonstrable effect on investment and exports; these actions included incentives to encourage reinvestment of corporate profits, reduction of the stamp tax, and expanding tariff rebates to include indirect exporters in the drawback system.

Tax treatment of small and medium-sized enterprises compared with share capital companies

Some details of the tax laws, company laws, and the capital market law in Egypt are worth highlighting here because of the mixed and confusing signals they may give to investors. These laws provide special tax benefits to large or joint-stock companies generally, or to those listed in the capital market as well as to the investors in such companies. They keep small businesses and partnerships subject to the taxes from which larger companies are exempted. At the same time, they impose special taxes on unlisted joint-stock companies. Consider the following examples mentioned in other chapters: a five-year tax exemption is extended only for companies employing fifty employees or more (provided they keep proper accounts); proprietorships and simple partnerships *(sociétés des personnes)*, unlike the normally larger joint-stock companies and limited liability companies, are not allowed to retain reserves before distribution of their net taxable profits; dividends on shares listed in the stock exchanges, and interest on bonds so listed, are exempt from the tax on movable capital and the general income tax; a notional interest on paid-in capital may be deducted from the tax base of the tax on the profits of joint-stock companies only; dividends received from investments in other companies may be deducted from the tax base of joint-stock companies; and amounts spent by individuals on the purchase of debt or equity may be deducted from the tax base provided they are invested in corporate firms only.

These exemptions and deductions clearly favor stock exchange companies and discriminate against the small 'personal' companies which account for most private enterprises in Egypt. However, other taxes discriminate against share-capital companies. An annual stamp tax is imposed on their share capital at the rate of 1.2 percent, of which shares listed in stock exchanges are now exempted. A capital gains tax (2 percent) is also imposed on securities of joint-stock companies which appear on official lists of the stock exchange market. The listing of private sector companies is limited to companies where subscribers are no fewer than 150 persons and where at least 30 percent of capital is subscribed by the public. The situation requires a review, at least to eliminate discrimination against small non-share-capital companies and to ensure standard tax treatment of the different instruments and types of investment, except when the need for special incentives is clearly established.

Real property law, registration, titling, and mortgage

While property law is generally well developed in Egypt, the title to real property is often difficult to define, especially as far as agricultural and desert land is concerned. This can have adverse effects on the business environment. Title to real property is established by law only through registration of the contract or the court decision transferring the property. Mainly due to the very high registration fees required by law, titles remain unregistered sometimes for generations. This not only creates unnecessary disputes; it also deprives the 'owner' of the ability to use the property as a collateral for bank credit. Excessive fees are also imposed on the mortgaging of real estate. Such excessive fees for the registration of titles and mortgages often lead to unsound practices such as the recording of lower-than-real prices in the deeds to be registered. They are usually coupled with time-consuming procedures applied by inefficient offices. Such problems are not of course limited to Egypt. But countries like Thailand and Mexico were able to improve greatly their land registration systems and have received financing from the World Bank both for technical assistance and for the buildings, facilities, and training needed for this purpose. As a result, they have succeeded in putting in place well functioning systems of real property registration, greatly stabilizing property relationships in rural areas.

Reform of the laws related to real property in Egypt must address the rent control issue in a manner that encourages once again building for rental purposes. An equitable solution can always be found to address existing contracts, as has been done in other countries. Ownership of real estate by non-Egyptians is also a subject that requires further analysis, with a view to encouraging investment and discouraging speculation.

Leasing and factoring

It is surprising that Egypt does not yet have a law on leasing operations in spite of the fact that a draft law was prepared for this purpose a decade ago. The 1985 draft law appears to be lacking in some important respects. It assumes that the lessor will always be a leasing company whereas it could also be the asset's manufacturer or a banking institution. It does not distinguish between the different types of leases and does not have special provisions on leveraged leases (or third-party lease) where part of the cost of the asset is borrowed by the lessor on a nonrecourse basis, the only collateral on the loan being the asset itself. Such special provisions are necessary in the context of Egyptian law which does not otherwise allow the mortgaging of movable assets not held by the creditor (nonpossessory securities). The draft law also provides, quite unjustifiably, for complete tax exemption for five years of the profits of leasing companies. It will be useful if the draft law is carefully reviewed and the appropriate legislation is issued without delay. Jordan, Morocco, and Tunisia have recently issued such laws.

A leasing law may also be complemented by legislation governing factoring operations. Factoring takes place when a manufacturer provides trade credit to the distributor so that the price of the product becomes due to the manufacturer only after delivery. The factor is a third party who provides risk assessment, credit risk-bearing, monitoring, and collection services. In certain cases, he may even act as ex post lender to meet short-term financing needs. The relationships involved can be complex from the accounting and tax treatment viewpoints and for this reason need to be clearly regulated. Factoring services are increasingly important in industrial countries and can be particularly useful in environments where credit collection is difficult. Their availability facilitates financing and trade transactions. A factoring law may therefore be opportune for a country like Egypt.

Social security laws and regulations

The comprehensive structural adjustment program under implementation in Egypt requires a comprehensive social safety net. The laws governing social security, medical insurance, and pension funds ought to be reviewed, with a view to ensuring the broadest possible coverage and the liberalization of investment of the funds involved to achieve the highest possible returns. These relatively huge funds can become the most active and diversified institutional investors in the country, injecting the economy with a new dynamism which it badly needs. In Chile a law was issued to permit enhanced participation of pension funds in equity markets which helped in energizing the capital market. In Bolivia, with World Bank support, independently managed mutual funds, financed through these institutional investors, are purchasing public sector companies and placing them under new management prior to selling them gradually to individuals and private entities. This intermediate step in the privatization process has been found to be helpful in a situation where direct extensive privatization was not practical.

Employment relations

Employment relationships, whether in the government, the public sector, or the private sector, are characterized by rigidity and excessive entitlements for employees at the expense of efficiency. The laws regulating civil service may also be comprehensively reviewed in the context of an overall administrative reform. Such a reform is needed, not only for the efficiency of government services, but also for private sector development. As the World Bank study on the so-called East Asian miracle revealed, an efficient and honest civil service is essential for a thriving private sector. France, for example, the country from which Egypt borrowed its administrative law and the *Conseil d'Etat* system, does not have the same degree of rigidity which characterizes Egyptian practices; this should be a priority area for legal reform. Employees' rights must, of course, be protected. This should not lead, however, to job entitlements for bad performers, extending equal treatment to unequal performers, or following a rule of absolute seniority, to mention only some of the malaise of existing practices.

CONCLUSION

The list of issues briefly mentioned in this chapter is of course not exhaustive. It nevertheless shows the broad scope of the required legal reform. This reform while relatively easy in terms of financial cost will require careful analysis and adequate consultation. It will also consume some political capital. But it should not be delayed. We know from experience that delay in carrying out reforms increases their costs, including the social and political costs. Early completion of the structural reforms and the legal and regulatory changes that need to accompany them will allow the government to concentrate on the developmental tasks that lie ahead, especially in improving the quality of education and other social services as well as the infrastructure.

In the final analysis, it is the quality of the individuals, the men and women who make the rules and run the institutions, which makes the difference. The working methods of these individuals and the services and facilities available to them are also of vital importance. Through economic and legal reforms Egypt will be able to do better in providing its people with high quality services and facilities. It will be better able to have a more efficient system for the management of its resources and to create an environment which enables its productive forces to achieve their promising potential and take full advantage of the new globalized markets.

Five

Labor Laws for Productivity Enhancement in Egypt

Hussein Ibrachy

INTRODUCTION

We are witnessing the end of a bipolar world. The triumph of representative democracies over totalitarian regimes, and of market-oriented economic systems over those centrally planned, accompanied the growth of multinational corporations to where they now account for one-third of total production assets globally. These trends have made competitiveness a *conditio sine qua non* of success. Although this concept is clear to most developing nations, some of them are galloping ahead, while others are severely lagging behind.

The economic strategy of Egypt has but one objective: enhancing production efficiency as the means to a better standard of living. It follows that labor legislation reform should compliment this strategy. The government must truly divest itself of the powers to interfere in the labor market. The government must be content in the role of an umpire and abandon intervention (often in the name of 'social peace'), or more precisely, it must relinquish control over labor relations.

In brief, the underlying theme of this chapter is 'reward and punishment,' combined with simultaneous contraction of the state's authority in the economic arena. Observation reveals that a major catalyst favoring the rapid progress in some countries as opposed to others stems from the extent of emphasis placed on the principle of 'reward and punishment'. While productivity is the central issue of concern in the realm of competitiveness, quality should always take precedence over quantity. Regretfully, in Egypt over the last four decades quantity has won, or more precisely, distorted figures thereof have prevailed.

THE EVOLUTION OF LABOR LEGISLATION IN EGYPT

Employee protection was nonexistent in Egypt in the early decades of the twentieth century; later, it was dealt with in a few scattered laws of minor impact. In the wake of the Egyptian Revolution, the president issued the first comprehensive legislation covering individual labor contracts. Law 317 of 1952 and Law 318 of 1952 addressed conciliation and arbitration; Law 319 is known as the Trade Union's Act; and Law 244 dealt with hiring unemployed workers. In 1959, the president issued Law 91—the Unified Code of Labor. It was interpreted in the way most protective of labor; social objectives overrode all other motivations. Nationalizations were sweeping the country, and private enterprise was being gradually crowded out, with severe repercussions on the gross national product (GNP).

In 1974, President Sadat introduced a new approach to economic development. He unequivocally advocated reliance on the private sector, which was to be on equal footing with the public sector. In the wake of the Arab and foreign investment law, labor law reform came into focus. The unified labor law (Law 137 of 1981) was meant to pave the way for cooperation of the two parties of production—the worker and the employer—for the benefit of the community and the people at large, without prejudice to either party. This is the law which has been applied for over thirteen years.

PROPOSED AMENDMENTS TO PRESENT LABOR LEGISLATION

A new labor law should, for the first time, clearly define the role of tripartite representation (government, employment, and employees) in labor relations; highlighted are the expected roles of collective bargaining and collective labor contracts. As a general rule, the Labor Department should have no role in individual labor relations. Barring exceptional cases, it should act as a catalyst or umpire in a team game evolving and arising from collective bargaining with a minimum level of protection of labor. For labor and/or employers' organizations, the courts should be the normal venue for addressing a grievance.

Investigation should be made into the possibility of renewing labor contracts for consecutive limited durations after their expiration. This idea has its critics (among them the ILO), who disapprove of workers being employed for limited durations, if the job itself is permanent. Under the present law, once a contract's duration is completed, an employer is 'stuck' with the employee, with little room to terminate his contract, even in cases where it would reasonably be warranted.

Recognition should be given to the right of labor organizations to strike, and of employers to lock out their businesses, partially or totally. The principle that the employer shall not be subject to 'corporeal' punishment, except when there is disregard for regulations pertaining to health and safety, should be explicitly established; penal sanctions should be clearly specified and should be deterrent.

Incidental leave should be deducted from the annual leave. The reason is that the average Egyptian employee already enjoys extended annual as well as weekly vacations and public holidays; if entitled to incidental leaves in addition, it would be detrimental to productivity. Currently, annual leave is three weeks, which is increased to one month after ten years of service. This is far too generous, and should be aligned with the country's international competitors.

'Reward and punishment' should be the underlying philosophy of any new labor legislation. A related issue is employers' freedom to hire and fire. If this prerogative is abused, delinquent employers should face the consequences in terms of a fair compensation. Also, if an employer is fully responsible for the conduct of employees, he cannot reasonably be denied the right to choose, supervise, and direct them. No public administrative authority should have power to suggest anybody for any job, unless requested to do so by the employer. This will shield the employer from being subjected to administrative pressure.

Law 137 of 1981 introduced a provision borrowed from the public sector: by virtue of its article 42, all private sector employees would receive an annual raise of 7 percent. This is an unfortunate tendency. Rather than equate public sector employees with the private sector, the legislature opted for the reverse (supposedly to offset inflation). The fact remains that every annual raise triggered a wave of inflation at a higher rate than the raise; in brief, the purchasing power of wages declined. Former French prime minister Raymond Barr sharply criticized a similar move by the former socialist government. He observed that general wage increments were invariably self-defeating. He emphasized that different industries do not necessarily have the same capacity to raise salaries, and probably not at the same time. Even within the same industry, not everyone can afford an imposed uniform raise. This is an area which should be left entirely to collective bargaining in each, or a given, industry.

Consideration should be given to providing more flexibility to employers in directing and reallocating staff. The current law does not seem to authorize the employer to reallocate work where necessary except in cases of safety enhancement and force majeure. If the employer is not authorized to reallocate work in case of need (for example if the worker's job were no longer needed) he or she may have no other choice than to terminate the contract employment, or to avoid hiring in the first place.

Under the present 1981 law, dismissal requires submission of the employer's dismissal decision to a tripartite consultative committee prior to enforcing the decision. Past experience has shown this consultative role to be futile and time-consuming. Prior to any dismissal, an employer, by virtue of article 71, is required to submit the case to the administrative body with judicial jurisdiction, presided over by a magistrate with four other members: a magistrate, a representative of the Labor Department, a business representative, and a labor representative. In practice, this proves a formidable obstacle to personnel management and labor mobility.

Finally, there is great confusion between penal offenses and disciplinary offenses in cases of dismissal of employees accused of a felony. The current law obliges employers to reinstate workers who have been suspended on grounds of having committed a felony if a court of law subsequently finds the employee innocent. Yet despite the past existence of this rule, courts have repeatedly deviated from it by 'praetorian action.' To illustrate the defect of the law, consider the following example—the case of a doorman of a burglarized factory who is accused of complicity but found innocent. During the trial, however, it is also established that he was asleep at the time of the offense. How could the employer possibly be compelled to reinstate him? The employer should have a free hand. If his decision, at the discretion of a court considering the case on its own merits, is unjustified, the employee would be entitled to fair compensation.

COLLECTIVE BARGAINING AND THE LEGISLATURE'S APPROACH TO FREEDOM OF ASSOCIATION

So far, we have dealt with labor relations as presently governed by Law 137 of 1981. However, two other major issues have been, and will remain, distinct, and covered by separate legislation—trade union organizations and social insurance, which are governed by Laws 35 and 79 of 1975, respectively. The government has repeatedly expressed its intention to introduce major reform to the latter two legislations, and every indication is that such reform is in the works. Here, we shall limit ourselves to the major issues, some of which might be resolved through amendments to the laws governing labor relations.

First of all, trade union movements in Egypt have not reached a stage of true emancipation. However, should they be recognized as a full partner in collective bargaining? There is some legitimate concern among employers as well as state authorities as to whether their rights and prerogatives in this regard should be bestowed upon them incrementally or all at one time.

In contrast, collective bargaining is a concept which causes much aggravation among employers; many cannot conceive how collective bargaining could contribute in any beneficial way to industry per se. Their chief concern revolves around the conviction that employees are too demanding. In reality, salary levels in Egypt are far below levels that would make raises financially threatening, provided, that is, that worker productivity increases. Employers should be prepared to give more as long as production efficiency is rising at a reasonable pace. It is hoped that over time, trade unions will, as has happened elsewhere, be true protectors of capitalism, rather than an eroding influence. Even the term 'privatization,' for which they harbored a significant degree of animosity, seems to be meeting greater acceptance. This growing acceptance has been further encouraged by a World Bank study which reflects that in rapidly developing nations, privatization contributed to, and accelerated movement toward, a better standard of living for labor as a whole, despite increased layoffs and early retirement plans.

It is an illusion to speak about labor relations with no representation for business. In Egypt, the only entities which currently have the right to speak on their behalf are the chambers of commerce and the Board of the Federation of Egyptian Industries (BFEI), the first being a governmental entity and the second quasi-governmental. Private sector employers have had no direct representation of their own. Employers in the private sector should have the right to have their own association. At present they are excluded from the general trade unions' law and are governed by special regulations under the unsuitable umbrella of the Ministry of Social Affairs. In effect, Law 35 of 1975 applies exclusively to trade unions.

It is noteworthy that a case concerning freedom of association and freedom of election was submitted to the ILO by the Syndicate of Engineering in March 1993 (case no. 170/1994). Although the petition was subsequently withdrawn by a newly elected board, the ILO decided the rules governing elections to the syndicate's board were a direct violation of the ILO's Conventions 87 and 98, which Egypt ratified in 1987.

SOCIAL INSURANCE

On the surface, it might appear as though employers would have little say in determining social insurance and security programs. On the contrary, however, they have substantial interest in subscribing to social insurance: economically secure workers are apt to be more productive than those who lack security.

During recent public hearings in Egypt dealing with social insurance reform, labor representatives voiced a harsh critique regarding investment in these social insurance funds. They felt the low rate of interest of current social insurance funds was unfair, bordering on shortchanging. They are right: the fact that those funds are administered by the state (and actually used by it to finance its public investment program) has deprived workers of the right to choose market-driven managers for their life savings. Not to mention the forgone sources of financing for more profitable private sector investments.

Another closely related issue which needs urgent attention and resolution is early retirement; it has been repeatedly mentioned by the media as a weapon to combat unemployment. Actual practice has shown this to be a fallacy; it has tended to cost far more than simply creating new jobs.

CONCLUSION

Employers feel the points listed in this paper are worthy of consideration in the elaboration of the amendments of new legislation regulating labor relations in the broad sense of the term. The main topics have been dealt with from an employer's perspective. A recent ILO report to the government of Egypt (April 1994) on necessary revisions to the labor law broadly coincides with the views expressed here, even when it addresses the issues from the point of view of aligning Egypt's legislation to its commitments under international conventions which it ratified and to which it is party.

The law has been examined here in a wider sense, and from a different angle—that of realizing our interests as employers and full partners of the tripartite representatives concerned with labor relations. Employers are the prospective investors in future development of the private sector. It is hoped that this paper will trigger fruitful discussions revolving around the basic issues of a complex problem—urgent revision of Egypt's labor laws.

Six

A PSD-Friendly Tax System

Hazem Hassan

INTRODUCTION

A quick glance at the Egyptian taxation system

The taxes and duties currently imposed in Egypt are divided into the following main categories:

a) Taxes on income, including:
   - Tax on profits of corporations (corporate tax)
   - Taxes on the incomes of individuals (personal income taxes), imposed on revenues from movable capital, industrial and commercial profits, revenues from free professions and other noncommercial professions, salaries and wages, and on revenues from real estate
   - Taxes and duties on revenues from buildings
   - Taxes and duties on revenues from agricultural land

b) Taxes on capital, including:
   - The proportional fiscal stamp tax on the capitals of companies
   - The inheritance tax

c) Taxes on transactions or disbursements, including:
   - Customs tax
   - Tax on sales
   - Fiscal stamp tax on documents and financial transactions
   - Sundry other taxes and duties

Taxes on income have the privilege of taking into consideration the contributory capacity of the taxpayer and are, therefore, more equitable than other types of taxes. However, income taxes have the disadvantage of being rather difficult to determine, assess, and collect. The taxes on capital are similar, to some extent, in their advantages and disadvantages to the income taxes. Usually, taxes on incomes and taxes on capital are referred to as direct taxes.

Taxes on transactions or disbursements, which are referred to as indirect taxes, do not usually take into consideration the contributory capacity of the taxpayer and, therefore, might not always be equitable. However, the procedures for determining, assessing, and collecting these indirect taxes are usually simpler than for direct taxes.

In Egypt, the General Tax Authority (GTA) carries out the determination, assessment, and collection of corporate taxes, personal income taxes, the stamp tax, and the inheritance tax. The Real Estate Tax Authority (RTA) determines, assesses, and collects the taxes on revenues of buildings and revenues derived from agricultural land; however, some governorates perform this function for themselves. The Customs Authority (CA) determines, assesses, and collects the customs tax, while the Tax on Sales Authority (TSA) determines, assesses, and collects the tax on sales. Other minor taxes and duties are collected by the appropriate government departments, for example, registration and notarization duties are collected by the Authority for Registration and Notarization.

Although social insurance contributions paid to the General Authority for Social Insurance are not technically considered to be taxes, they do represent an important source of revenue for the State Treasury and are, therefore, considered as quasi taxes.

General review of the economics of the Egyptian taxation system

The burden of taxes and other sovereign revenues in relation to the gross domestic product (GDP) of Egypt has increased in recent years. Thus, the ratio of the taxes and other sovereign revenues to GDP in 1991/92 was 18.6 percent; this rose to 21.8 percent in the following year, and further to 23.2 percent in 1993/94. If this ratio is computed solely on the basis of taxes, excluding other sovereign revenues, the tax burden ratio for 1993/94 would be 20.8 percent.

Comparing these ratios with a sample of other countries, we find that the tax burden ratio in Egypt is less than that in advanced countries but higher than that in other developing countries: USA 34 percent; UK 35 percent; France 44 percent; Indonesia 13 percent; Malaysia 20 percent; South Korea 15 percent. Since the average per capita income in Egypt is considerably lower than those of the countries mentioned in the comparison, it would appear that the tax burden ratio in Egypt is somewhat high.

The Egyptian taxation system relies more on indirect taxes than direct taxes in financing the state budget because indirect taxes are

Table 6-1
Direct and indirect taxes as percentage of total taxes in selected countries

Country	Direct taxes	Indirect taxes
Egypt	36	64
US	77	23
UK	65	35
Indonesia	51	49
Malaysia	40	60

easier to determine, assess, and collect, though, as already mentioned above, they are less equitable than direct taxes.

Comparing the percentages of direct taxes and indirect taxes to total taxes of Egypt with those of a sample of advanced and developing countries, we find that most of these countries depend to a greater extent on direct taxes to finance their budgets, as seen in Table 6-1. In recent years, the Egyptian budget has suffered from the structural imbalances of the Egyptian economy; this has led to an increasing deficit in the budget. The percentage of the budget deficit to the GDP in 1987/88 was 32 percent. This caused the Egyptian government to start implementing an economic reform program which brought about a decrease in the budget deficit to 6.9 percent in 1991/92 and to 5.3 percent in 1992/93. The rate of inflation dropped considerably from 21 percent in 1989/90 to 9.7 percent in 1991/92, and is still decreasing. The exchange rate of the Egyptian pound vis-à-vis strong foreign currencies has remained stable during the economic reform period, in spite of all the internal problems. Also, the dependence of the government on foreign sources in financing the budget deficit has declined. All this is considered to be a definite success of the Egyptian economic reform program. This success was brought about by increasing the tax revenues, reducing public spending, and resorting more to treasury bills in financing the budget deficit. In the area of taxes the economic reform program was able to increase tax revenues from LE9.8 billion in 1988/89 to LE24.2 billion in 1991/92. Most of this increase in revenues came from the corporate tax, the proceeds of which have risen from LE2.9 billion to LE8.3 billion; the sales tax, or ex-consumption tax, the income from which rose from LE2.4 billion to LE6.6 billion; and the customs tax, which increased from LE2.8 billion to LE4.8 billion. Concerning taxes on incomes of individuals, revenues are still relatively small, but have increased from LE430 million in 1988/89, to LE840 million in 1991/92.

General evaluation of the tax regime–economic policy and suggestions for further reform

Any economic reform process is accompanied by some negative aspects, which are, in fact, the price that must be paid for such reform. The negative aspects of Egypt's economic reform program have manifested themselves in a state of recession accompanied by a rise in the lending interest rate, an increase in the unemployment rate, and a slowdown in investment in both the public and private sectors. It is also feared that if the government continues to expand the issuance of the treasury bills, this might lead to excessive increase in the domestic public debt; the cost of serving this debt may cause, in turn, an increased budget deficit, with an increase in the issuance of money and a rise in the inflation rate.

In order to avoid this vicious cycle, the government should proceed in two parallel directions. First, reduce the public expenditure, or at least freeze it at its present level. One of the methods of doing this is to reemploy surplus manpower in government departments and in the public sector in productive jobs, thereby benefiting the workers and society as a whole. Other methods include more rationing of the government subsidies and decreasing gradually the interest rate on treasury bills. Second, increase public revenues. The most common method adopted by the government to increase public revenues is to increase tax revenues. However, increasing tax revenues is a double-edged sword which could overburden the taxpayers, cause discontent, and discourage investment. It is, therefore, necessary in this regard to apply several important reform methods in a harmonized manner, the most important of which are the following. First, identify the taxpayers very strictly, particularly to expand the base of taxpayers subject to the personal income taxes, who are still playing a very limited role in financing the budget. Second, improve the efficiency of the tax administration so that it becomes expeditious and more equitable in assessing and collecting taxes, and in resolving tax disputes. It is also suggested that a public relations department be set up in the Tax Authority similar to the 'reception office' in the French tax administration, which performs services for the taxpayers in solving their problems, guiding them, and reinstating confidence in their relationship with the French tax administration. Third, depend more on direct taxes rather than on indirect taxes in increasing the tax revenues, on the principle that the direct taxes are fairer and take into consideration the contributory ability of the taxpayer, especially as we have seen that the tax burden ratio has risen in recent years until it reached 23.2 percent in 1993/94.

Tax exemptions should be restructured in correlation with reducing the tax rates and abolishing some taxes such as the state resources tax. At present Egypt has many tax exemptions prescribed by numerous laws, such as the investment law, the new urban communities law, and the tourism and reconstruction laws, in addition to exemptions contained in the tax legislation itself. Although these tax exemptions formed a most important incentive for investment in Egypt during the past twenty years, with the elapse of this long period, it has become necessary to reconsider matters. Allowing projects that will be established in the future—when the State Treasury will need more revenues to reduce the budget deficit—to enjoy the same generous tax exemptions prescribed in the present laws could drive the government to increase the tax burdens on the taxpayers to a degree that is unacceptable or unbearable. Hence, tax exemptions need to be restructured and rationalized. For example, it is not feasible that a new urban community will remain 'new' indefinitely, because after the lapse of fifteen or twenty years from its foundation, it will have completed its growth or moved a considerable way toward this end and thus it is neither logical nor beneficial to the national economy to continue giving ten-year tax exemptions to projects that will be established there. In such cases, tax exemptions should be reduced, canceled, or gradually phased out, for example, over five years for projects of vital importance, over three years for less important projects, and so on. By this and other similar means, the government will be able to increase tax revenues from new projects without burdening existing projects and taxpayers in general. In view of the importance of this subject, it is addressed in more detail later in this chapter.

THE CORPORATE TAX

The corporate tax is an annual tax imposed on the overall net profit of any corporation operating in Egypt, irrespective of the purpose of the corporation, and including the profits resulting from any overseas activity, unless this activity is in the form of an independent entity. The corporations referred to in the law include joint-stock companies, partnerships limited by shares, and limited liability companies. The tax also applies to banks, public sector companies and corporations, and branches of foreign companies with respect to the profits realized from their activities in Egypt. The following is a review of the key problems in regard to corporate taxation that companies operating in Egypt face today, as well as recommendations for solving them.

The rate. The tax rate on the profits of corporations is 40 percent, with the exception of profits of industrial companies and profits resulting from export operations, for which the tax rate is 32 percent. In the case of the profits of companies searching for oil and producing it, the tax rate is 40.55 percent. The taxable income of companies and other types of corporations mentioned above is also subject to an additional tax called "development of state resources duty," the rate of which is 2 percent imposed on the part of any profit exceeding LE18,000 per annum. Table 6-2 compares the rate of the Egyptian corporate tax and the rates in some advanced and developing countries, from which it is apparent that the standard rate of the Egyptian corporate tax, being 40 percent plus 2 percent state resources duty, is relatively high and should be reduced to a maximum of 30 percent.

The tax authority/taxpayer relationship. Taxpayers suffer from many problems and disputes with the Tax Authority as a result of the failure of many working in the Tax Administration to comprehend the true role of taxes in the society; taxes represent the state's share in the profits and incomes of citizens and companies, and should be computed in accordance with proper and equitable concepts provisioned in the tax law. Yet a large part of the personnel in the Tax Authority, in particular examining and collecting inspectors, consider the Tax Authority as a system for collection of funds per se. Furthermore, they regard inflexibility and the erroneous application of the provisions of the tax law as a legitimate means to realize this purpose.

Table 6-2
Corporate tax rate in selected countries (percentage)

Country	Rate
Egypt	
standard rate	40
industrial and export activities	32
oil exploration and production	40.55
USA	15 to 38
France	33.33
UK	33
Indonesia	15 to 35
Malaysia	32

As a result, thousands of disputes between the Tax Authority and taxpayers have taken place, representing numerous amendments to tax returns which have no basis or substantiation. Income items are increased, and expenses and charges are disallowed in a random manner by tax inspectors, with no supporting evidence of their ineligibility, in order to arrive at an amount of taxable profit which is many times greater than the amount stated on the tax return. Solving these disputes requires great effort on the part of both the business sector and the Tax Authority, and precious time is wasted in the internal committees, appeals committees, and courts of law.

Therefore, it is necessary to institute radical change in the tax system, implemented by teaching the tax laws in their proper contexts to personnel working in the Tax Authority. The personnel in the Tax Authority should be guided by accuracy in applying the tax law, together with flexibility and ease in application.

It is also the duty of the senior supervisors in the Tax Authority to continuously supervise their assistants and to furnish them with the necessary interpretative instructions. The supervisors should arrange ongoing training sessions for assistants and apply a system of punishment and reward relevant to job performance; otherwise the sums collected in taxes will represent the only yardstick used in judging the performance of tax inspectors.

General provisions. Among the most important internationally established accounting principles is the right of companies and firms to make provisions to meet any probable losses in asset values, which are difficult to evaluate with any degree of accuracy, and also to cover any liabilities or financial burdens, which are also difficult to determine accurately. These calculations should be taken into account before the determination of net profit. These accounting principles state that such provisions should be made even if operations show a loss. The present tax law adopted the principle that provisions should be a deductible cost, but it imposed two restrictions as to what should be allowable costs: 1) provisions that are made to meet losses or financial burdens that are certain to occur; and 2) the total annual provisions should not exceed 5 percent of the annual net profit of the company.

Because of these two constraints, provisions can be approved only as an allowable cost within the narrowest limits. During tax audits, provisions formed by the company are often rejected on the grounds they do not cover losses or financial burdens that are, from the point of view of the Tax Authority, certain to occur. Also, the second condition (within 5 percent of net profit) results in companies that are encountering financial difficulties and realizing meager profits not being able to gain approval for the greater portion of their provisions because they usually exceed 5 percent of net profit. In the case of companies that incur losses, such provisions are not approved at all. Consequently we find that many companies are obliged to pay a corporate tax although their accounts show losses or meager profits because of disallowing their provisions.

It is recommended that the tax law be amended: provisions should be considered as allowable costs to be deducted, without specifying a certain percentage of net profit, as long as there is available sufficient proof supporting the necessity for these provisions (that is, not necessarily certain to occur), and as long as the estimate of their value is within reasonable limits. Furthermore, a 'doubtful debts' provision, for debts whose collection is doubtful, should be approved as an allowable cost on condition that there is convincing proof and evidence supporting its formation, and its estimation is within reason and such that the balance of said provision at the end of each year does not exceed 15 percent of the total value of the debts due to the company.

Bank provisions to meet credit risks. As already indicated, the tax law places restrictions on what could be considered as legitimate deductions from revenues. It is regrettable that banks, as financial institutions that are most sensitive to market conditions and to various economic changes, are the institutions most severely affected by these tax restrictions imposed on provisions. This is because banks need to devise adequate provisions to meet doubtful or troubled loans and debts, and credit risks in general.

The Central Bank of Egypt sets the guidelines in the banking industry concerning accounting procedures and what provisions must and can be made; however, banks are treated in this regard in the same way as companies and commercial firms. Their provisions or a large portion of their provisions to meet credit risks are rejected, and the banks are forced as a result to pay a corporate tax on the amount of these provisions which have been fiscally disallowed.

It is notable that paragraph 6 of article 114 of the tax law, which deals with the subject of provisions, has given due consideration to insurance companies. It states that they shall be exempted from the restrictions imposed on the provisions referred to. Thus the technical provisions which the insurance companies are obliged to form in pursuance of the provisions of Insurance Law 10 of 1981 are tax deductible without any restrictions or limits. This constitutes an admission by the legislator that the true net profit of the insurance company cannot be arrived at without deducting the technical provisions from revenues.

No doubt that banks are similar to the insurance companies in that, ultimately, provisions have to be formed in order to arrive at the true net profit and financial position. The technical provisions in insurance companies are comparable with the doubtful debts provisions in banks. Both banks and insurance companies are financial institutions that are highly sensitive to the economic cycle and systemic risks. Consideration should be given to amending the tax law, allowing for full exemptions from restrictions concerning the deduction of bad debt provisions by banks, as long as these provisions are formed according to the rules set by the Central Bank of Egypt and generally accepted accounting standards.

Interest accrual and nonperforming loans. Accepted accounting standards in banking require that interest on any loans and advances encountering difficulties not be recorded in the bank's profit and loss account but should be either suspended in a special account to be included on the liabilities side of the balance sheet or not recorded at all. In other words, the interest on such loans and advances should not be recorded in the profit and loss account except when collected.

There are instructions issued by the Central Bank of Egypt to all the banks operating in Egypt requiring them to apply the above-mentioned rules in recording interests on loans and advances that are delinquent or nonperforming. The objective of this accounting treatment is not to inflate the bank's profits with untrue or uncollectible revenues.

However, the tax law has not given due consideration to the nature of the banking activity, and it has been customary in the tax administration to treat banks as other commercial companies are treated, without discrimination. Hence, the Tax Authority refuses to accept the principle of nonaccrual of interest and insists on adding this interest to the banks' revenues and subjecting it to the corporate tax. This tax treatment of nonaccrual of interest leads to negating the effect which proper accounting standards wish to realize. The outcome of making the banks pay corporate tax on this untrue revenue is to make the banks' loss twofold: losing that interest plus bearing the tax on it at the rate of 42 percent.

Law 187 of 1993. This law, which amends some provisions of Tax Law 157 of 1981, imposed a tax for the first time on certain revenues, among which are the revenues from movable capital that is part of the property of the company but that is not connected directly with the company's main activity. When it comes to the practical application of this new provision, the expression "not connected directly with the company's activity" raises many problems. For instance, in some companies the interest on time deposits with banks could be considered as connected with their main activity, whereas in some other companies it would be considered as not related to their main activity. The Tax Authority should study this subject with the several parties involved as soon as possible, in order to avoid any problems in applying this new provision of the tax law.

Article 120/4: Equality in tax exemptions. Article 120/4 (bis) of the tax law allows companies to deduct from their taxable profit an amount equal to 90 percent of the dividends received on their investment in a joint-stock company on condition that this company has paid the corporate tax due on its profit or is exempt therefrom.

The objective of article 120/4 (bis) is to avoid paying a corporate tax on the same income twice. However, this article ignored dividends received on investments in companies other than joint-stock companies, that is, partnerships limited by shares and limited liability companies, and this will result in subjecting the dividends of these two types of companies to the corporate tax twice; firstly, the dividends as part of the profit of the company invested in are subjected to the corporate tax, and secondly, the dividends are received by the investing company and included in its taxable profit subject to the corporate tax. This constitutes a double taxation, as well as a gross inequality in the tax treatment of the dividends received from joint-stock companies as compared to the dividends received from the other types of companies.

Article 120/4 (bis) should be amended such that an amount equal to 90 percent of the dividends received by a company on its investment in a partnership limited by shares or from a limited liability company shall be deducted from the taxable profit of the investing company.

Amending article 120/1 of the tax law. This article allows joint-stock companies whose shares are listed at the stock exchange to deduct from their taxable profit an amount equal to the interest on their paid-up capital at the prevailing interest rate on time deposits with banks.

This tax allowance is limited to listed joint-stock companies. Partnerships limited by shares, limited liability companies, as well as foreign branches, all of which cannot list in the stock exchanges, do not enjoy this tax allowance even though they are subject to the same income tax treatment applicable to joint-stock companies and are subject to the proportional stamp tax on their capital. This represents discrimination in the treatment of joint-stock companies as compared with the other types of companies. Article 120/1 should be amended to permit all companies to deduct an amount equal to the interest on their capital mentioned above.

Article 111 and double taxation. Paragraph 3 of article 111 (bis) states that the corporate tax shall be imposed at the rate of 32 percent on amounts received by companies as commissions or brokerage not related to their main activity, on royalties for their knowhow, and on performance rights, whether such amounts are realized in Egypt or abroad.

Since such revenues are normally included in the profit and loss account of the companies receiving them, and the tax law did not provide for their deduction from the taxable profit of these companies, this leads to double taxation: the first time on receiving the revenue as it will be subject to the withholding tax at the indicated rate of 32 percent, and the second time when this revenue is included in the company's taxable profit subject to the corporate tax at the rate of 40 percent.

To avoid the double taxation referred to above, Tax Law 157 of 1981 needs to be amended. This may be done by either adding a new clause to article 120/4 (bis) allowing for the complete deduction of the revenues referred to above from the taxable income of the company receiving them, or amending article 118 of the tax law to provide for the deduction of 90 percent of such revenues from the taxable profit of the company receiving them.

Reducing the Tax Burden in Correlation with Restructuring Tax Exemptions. In an attempt to compensate for the deficit in the state sovereign resources, the Egyptian government has recently imposed more direct and indirect taxes, the most important of which are the following: doubling sales tax; doubling the proportional and the specific stamp tax; maintaining a high tax rate (reaching 48 percent) on the types of income (other than salaries and income from movable property) subject to the unified income tax; imposing the state resources development duty; levying taxes on profits derived from carrying out commercial and professional activity outside Egypt without taking into consideration the principle of territoriality; levying a tax on the salaries of employees working abroad; and insisting on not reducing the high rate of corporate tax.

Perhaps tax burdens could be reduced and tax exemptions restructured; the following suggest some possibilities. On reducing tax burdens, (i) abolish the proportional stamp tax on issued share capital of companies; (ii) reduce the progressive tax rates imposed on the individual's total income (other than wages and salaries), i.e., the tax on profits from commercial and industrial activities, income from liberal professions (self-employed professionals), and income from real estate. The maximum rate should be 30 percent, which would be acceptable to the taxpayers; (iii) reduce the proportional and the specific stamp taxes on transactions; (iv) abolish the state resources development duty; (v) grant profits derived from export a full tax exemption; (vi) apply a reduced tax rate to profits retained by companies and used in upgrading their productive assets; and (vii) abolish tax on the salaries of employees working abroad.

There are also numerous corporate tax exemptions granted for projects under various laws (see Table 6-3). To balance the required reduction in tax burdens with the genuine needs of the state budget, there must also be a restructuring of the system of exemptions. The tax exemption periods should vary according to the nature of the project, its importance to the economy, and its contribution to solving the unemployment problem. For instance, the tax exemption period for projects in the industrial sector, particularly heavy industries, should be longer in comparison with that granted to hospitals and medical centers or the tourism sector and so on. Also, exemptions should not be granted to the projects in a specific sector which are no longer

Table 6-3
Periods of tax exemption for projects established under various laws

Tax exemption	Period (years)
For projects established under the Investment Law	5–10
For projects established under the New Urban Communities Law	10
For hotels and touristic projects	5–10
For projects in the new industrial cities and remote areas	10
For industrial projects which employ fifty employees or more	5
For land reclamation and cultivation projects	10
For reclamation and cultivation of desert land projects	10
For poultry breeding, cattle ranches, and fisheries	5–10
For free zones projects	life of project

needed or which do not help in solving the unemployment problem. In fact, tax exemptions and exemption periods granted for new projects in the various sectors should be reviewed every three years, in light of changing economic and market conditions.

A new and different type of tax exemption should be devised, not in the form of exemption from tax for a number of years, but in the form of a tax credit the amount of which is calculated as a percentage of the invested capital and to be used within a specific number of years in payment of tax liabilities. This type of exemption is more suitable for projects such as hotels and tourism, whose operations are exposed to considerable fluctuations due to the influence of political and external factors, as well as for example for heavy industry projects, which do not reach the profitable stage until several years have passed.

It would be more suitable if the extent of the tax exemption in the earlier years of the project differs from that in the later years, so that projects would be given full exemption in the earlier years then partial and declining exemption later. The tax exemption period should differ from one industrial city to another depending on its geographical location. For example, projects in new industrial cities in Upper Egypt should enjoy longer exemption periods than those established in the Tenth of Ramadan City, Sixth of October City, and so on. Also, exemptions should not be given to projects in the new communities once the community has reached the required level of development.

The five-year tax exemption granted to partnerships in the industrial field when converted into companies according to article 120/8 of the tax law should be conditional on injecting new capital into the company and increasing its productive capacity and number of employees.

Reducing the tax burdens in the manner described above, simultaneously with the restructuring of the tax exemptions granted under the various laws, will not reduce the state sovereign resources and will have positive impact on the country's economic development and on its current unemployment problem.

TAX ON INCOMES OF INDIVIDUALS

Since the imposition of the income tax system in Egypt by Law 14 of 1939, and until recently, Egypt applied a system of multiple taxation by imposing a separate tax on each type of income: a tax on revenues from movable capital or property; a tax on industrial and commercial profits; a tax on salaries and wages; and a tax on the revenues of free and noncommercial professions.

Law 99 of 1949 further imposed a general income tax on the total annual income of the individual, supplementing the other taxes referred to above. After that, Law 157 of 1981 was issued to replace both Law 14 of 1939 and Law 99 of 1949; it retained the system of multiple taxes, except that it excluded corporations from being subject to industrial and commercial profits tax and devoted a separate section entitled "corporate profit tax" for the profit tax on companies and other types of corporations.

The system of multiple taxation has been criticized by many specialized researchers because it often leads to unfairness and inequality in fiscal treatment across taxpayers, in spite of the fact that their total incomes may be equal. Advanced countries relinquished the multiple tax system a long time ago and instead adopted the unified income tax system.

Egyptian legislators responded favorably to the demand that the multiple tax system be changed by issuing Law 187 of 1993, which amended Law 157 of 1981 by canceling the multiple tax system and adopting the unified tax system on incomes of individuals. According to the new system, commercial and industrial profits, revenues from free and noncommercial professions, and revenues from real estate became subject to the unified tax. The moveable capital revenues are still subject to a separate specific tax at the rate of 32 percent. Also the legislature excluded salaries and wages from the unified tax, and imposed on them a tax rate whose scale was lower than that of the unified tax.

When Law 187 of 1993 was issued, the government stated that the new system was considered to be an important step toward the comprehensive application of the unified tax system in its proper meaning. The following are, however, the most important flaws in the unified tax law, and some recommendations for remedying them.

Residence and taxation. Article 3 of Law 157 of 1981, after its amendment by Law 187 of 1993, introduced a new definition of residence, which stipulated that a person is considered as a resident for tax purposes in Egypt (a) if he resides in Egypt for a period exceeding 183 days either continuously or at intervals during any one fiscal year; (b) if Egypt is his principal place of residence; (c) if Egypt is the location of the head office for the management of his business; or (d) if Egypt is the center of his commercial, industrial, or professional activities. If a person is regarded as a resident, all revenues accruing to that person, of whatever description and whether earned in Egypt or abroad, including income from any overseas investments, shall be subject to income tax in Egypt.

The first item (a) above will likely result in double taxation because the revenues earned abroad by foreign nationals will be subject to taxes both in his own country and in Egypt at the same time. Because of this unfair definition of 'resident,' foreign nationals will either be deterred from working in Egypt, thereby depriving the country of much needed expertise, or they will accept jobs in Egypt by demanding very high remuneration to compensate for the double taxation burden.

In this respect it should be indicated that paragraph 2 of article 4 of the tax law exempts foreign technicians or experts from taxation on revenues earned outside of Egypt. However, it has been our experience, that the Tax Authority does not take a simple view of the term 'foreign expert.' The Tax Authority narrowly defines a foreign expert as one who comes to Egypt for a specific and temporary assignment. This does not cover foreign nationals who occupy positions in companies or institutions in Egypt. In order to prove that they are eligible for tax exemption, such persons must submit to the Tax Authority a certificate from the Ministry of Manpower stating that they are foreign experts. In practice, this, together with other impediments to gaining this exemption, prevents foreign experts in the final analysis from enjoying any of the tax exemptions or benefits provided by law.

If we consult international agreements on the prevention of double taxation for guidance in defining residency, we find that most of them apply the following standards. First, a person is considered to be resident in the country where he has a permanent domicile at his disposal. If he has a permanent home at his disposal in both states between which a double taxation prevention agreement has been concluded, he shall be considered as resident in the state in which he has stronger personal or economic relations, and which is the center of his vital interests. Second, in case the person does not have a permanent domicile at his disposal in any of the two contracting states or in case it is not possible to determine the state in which the center of the person's vital interests exist, he shall be considered as resident of the state where he has a usual place of residence. Third, if the person's usual place of residence is in both contracting states, or if he does not have a usual place of residence in any of the two states, he shall be considered as resident of the state whose nationality he holds.

Item (a) of article 3 of the income tax law, which states that a foreign national will be considered as resident for tax purposes if he resides in Egypt for more than 183 days in any one year, conflicts with international conventions and with the provisions of the international agreements for the prevention of double taxation. Therefore, canceling this item and confining the definition of 'residency' to those points mentioned in items (b), (c), and (d) of article 3, as referred to above, should be considered.

Commercial and industrial profits: Inequality of tax treatment between the industrial companies and industrial partnerships. Law 157 of 1981, as amended by Law 187 of 1993, provides for the exemption of any industrial company employing fifty or more workers from the corporate tax for a period of five years. The tax law did not grant a similar exemption to industrial partnerships or enterprises that are subject to the unified tax even if they employ fifty or more workers. This is an unjustifiable discrimination in tax treatment. If the state wants to encourage industry, this encouragement of industry should not be linked with the legal form of the industrial establishment.

Industrial partnerships and enterprises employing fifty or more workers should be granted exemption from the unified tax on income for five years provided they keep proper books of account. This accords them tax treatment similar to that given to industrial companies and would encourage industry in general.

Commissions and royalties. Tax Law 157 of 1981, as amended by Law 187 of 1993, subjects all amounts paid to any individual or partnership—either in the form of commission or brokerage that is not directly related to his profession—and also any amount paid as royalty, to the unified income tax at the progressive rate provided for in article 90 of the law, without any deductions for costs incurred or family allowances. The law obliges the payer of the commission or brokerage, and also the payer of the royalty, to calculate the tax, deduct it at source, and remit it to the Tax Authority. There is no justification for subjecting casual commissions and royalties to the unified tax at its progressive rate separately without deducting from either of them any costs or amounts for family allowance. This is unfair and is a deviation from the unified tax system.

Deduction and addition at source. Tax Law 157 of 1981, as amended by Law 187 of 1993, continued to apply the system of deduction and addition at source on account of taxes, in spite of the following problems which this system causes.

First, the minimum level of the amount of the transaction which is subject to the deduction and addition at source is LE10. This has not been changed since the system was first introduced about twenty years ago. This means that the majority of transactions will be subject to the deduction and addition at source system, which entails the expenditure of a considerable amount of time, effort, and money by all parties required to implement this system. The minimum amount of the transaction subject to the deduction and addition system should be raised from LE10 to LE200. However, for amounts less than LE200 a simple form could be provided to the parties implementing the system by which they could notify the Tax Authority via a central department therein.

Second, the deduction and addition at source system requires filling out specific forms which must be sent to the relevant tax inspectors in the various areas at monthly or quarterly intervals, accompanied by the proceeds of the deductions and additions. Completing these forms takes so much time and effort that some companies devote special sections of their organizational structure to dealing solely with the withholding system (deductions and additions).

Third, practical application of the withholding system has indicated that the rates of deduction and addition are, in many cases, high and do not take into consideration the true profit ratios of the taxpayers. The relatively high deduction or addition percentages lead to amounts being remitted to the Tax Authority on account of income taxes greatly in excess of the amounts actually due from the taxpayers. Obtaining a refund of amounts settled in excess requires extensive time and effort. Therefore, some taxpayers have debit balances due from the Tax Authority, the amounts of which increase year after year, without repayment or response. Professional firms present a clear example of this problem. A periodic review should be made of the deduction and addition percentages for various activities, and on the basis of this review, the percentages should be amended to conform with realistic ratios of net profit in each type of activity. This should result in the amounts remitted to the Tax Authority according to the withholding system being reasonably less than the actual income taxes due. Law 187 of 1993 required the representative offices of foreign companies to implement the withholding system, although these offices do not engage in any commercial activity, and their work is confined to the study of the Egyptian market. In view of the limited activity of the representative offices, they usually employ only a small number of staff often not exceeding two persons . Obliging such offices to comply with the withholding system is an exhausting demand on them because they are not equipped to implement it. Representative offices should be exempted from applying the withholding at source system.

Salaries and wages tax: Excluding salaries and wages from the taxable income subject to the unified tax. The tax law, as amended, gave special consideration to salaries when determining the net amount subject to tax. Numerous deductions and allowances were given to salaries only, and not to other forms of income, with the intention of protecting those earning small or limited salaries. Furthermore, the law removed salaries and wages from the taxable income subject to the unified tax and subjected them to the income tax separately at a progressive rate lower than that of the unified tax. This rate is 20 percent on salaries up to LE50,000 per annum and 32 percent on brackets of salaries in excess of that amount.

While the first part of privileges related to the deductions and allowances is justified in that it protects the earners of small and limited salaries, the second part, relating to subjecting the salaries to separate income tax of less progressive rate, benefits people earning high salaries (often exceeding the incomes of persons engaged in commercial, industrial, and free professions) and therefore not in need of special treatment.

More allowances to salary earners. In addition to the point raised above, concerning the possibility of granting salary earners more tax deductions and allowances provided that their salaries are to be included in the individual's total income subject to the unified tax, there are two important kinds of basic costs which could be added to the allowances—medical expenses and school fees. This should not be controversial: the tax law should prescribe a reasonable allowance for school fees and another allowance for medical expenses if they exceed a certain limit.

Exemption of casual workers. The tax law exempts the wages of casual workers from the income tax on condition that the workers are not employed on a permanent basis and do not have another source of income. This new provision has the following disadvantages. First, it granted the exemption without specifying a maximum wage that could be tax free. Before the tax law was amended, taxes were levied on the wages of casual workers on amounts exceeding LE6 per day. There is no doubt that this was fairer since it would be unreasonable to exempt from tax the wage of a casual worker earning LE20 or more per day.

Second, concerning the condition which requires that the casual worker not be employed on a permanent basis, criteria should be laid down clearly defining what constitutes temporary employment and what constitutes permanent employment. In fact, some disputes have recently arisen between the Tax Authority and contracting companies regarding this very point.

Criteria need to be established as to when an employee should be considered permanent. For example, after six or twelve months of employment at the same job, a worker should be considered to be employed on a permanent basis and should be treated in the same way as a permanent employee as far as taxes are concerned.

Finally, the condition that the casual worker should not have another source of income is a strange one. If we know that the employer is required by law to compute the tax and withhold it from the worker's pay, how could the employer possibly ascertain whether or not the worker had another source of income? To avoid confusion, it is worth considering a return to the provision of the tax law before the 1993 amendment (that the wage of a casual worker should be subject to tax if it exceeds a specific amount, say LE10 per day) and the cancellation of the condition that the worker should not have another source of income.

Revenues from the practice of free and noncommercial professions: Comparing the tax treatment of revenues from professions with that of salaries. Although both the free profession practitioner and the salaried employee earn their incomes by working, the amended tax law granted salary earners many tax deductions and allowances which it did not grant to the free profession practitioners. Furthermore, the tax rate on salaries stops at 32 percent, while the unified tax rate on revenues of free professions could reach 48 percent. This differentiation in tax treatment is unfair.

It was mentioned above that the deduction and addition rates should be reviewed periodically and amended in such a way as to be more realistic. In this respect, article 74 of the tax law stipulates that the deduction at source of amounts paid to the free professions practitioners is 10 percent on amounts less than LE500 and 15 percent on amounts exceeding LE500.

Experience has shown that, in the case of large professional firms such as accounting, legal, or engineering consulting firms, applying these rates results in amounts withheld at source in excess of the taxes actually due from them and these excesses accumulate at the Tax Authority while the proprietors of these firms find great difficulty when trying to obtain refunds. This affects the liquidity of the firms and could, in fact, be considered as an additional tax unfairly imposed on them. The government should reduce the rate of deduction at source for practitioners of free professions and for noncommercial earners such that it does not exceed 5 percent of the amount paid to them.

The recently amended tax law also introduced a new article (66) which requires the application of the unified tax to the net income resulting from exercising the free professions abroad if the head office or permanent domicile for practicing the activity is located in Egypt. This new provision does not clearly define the tax treatment for cases in which the free profession practitioner has a center for practicing his activity in Egypt and another center for practicing the activity abroad independent of the center in Egypt, permanently established, and subject to tax or the tax system in the state in which it operates. The obscurity of the text in this case may result in unfair double taxation and discourage the practitioners of free professions from establishing offices abroad. We therefore recommend that the foreign activity of the practitioner of the free profession should not be subjected to the income tax in Egypt if such activity assumes the form of a permanent independent office abroad, just as is the case with commercial and industrial enterprises according to article 16 of the same law.

The high progressive rate of the unified tax. In spite of the fact that the tax law, after adopting the unified tax system, somewhat reduced the progressive tax rate on incomes of individuals compared with the rates levied under the multiple tax system with a general income tax, the unified tax rate is still high. It starts at 20 percent and ends at 48 percent for incomes over LE68,000 per year; in addition, there is the state resources development duty at the rate of 2 percent on amounts in excess of LE18,000 per annum, bringing the upper limit of the tax rate to 50 percent. For comparison, personal income taxes in some advanced and developing countries are as follows: UK 20–40 percent; France 12–56.8 percent; Indonesia 15–35 percent; Malaysia 2–34 percent; South Korea 5–45 percent. Thus, with the exception of France, the rates of personal income taxes are lower in these countries than in Egypt. If we take into consideration that the levels of incomes per capita in these countries are significantly higher than those in Egypt, it becomes abundantly clear that the burden of the personal income tax in Egypt is abnormally heavy. The high rate of the unified tax in Egypt could result in one of two things. The first is partnerships converting themselves into companies, since the tax rate for the companies does not exceed 32 percent to 40 percent. In addition to that, listed joint-stock companies enjoy an allowance equal to the notional interest on capital computed at the interest rate on time deposits at the rate prevailing during the year. However, it is noticed that the cost of conversion is high and cannot be afforded by every partnership. The second potential result is that an unduly heavy burden could be placed on some small industries, and small craftsmen and workshops, which the state is endeavoring to activate and encourage, and this may lead them to evade the tax or to direct their activities to other countries.

The progressive rate of the unified tax should be reconsidered and reduced so as to start at 15 percent and end at 30 percent as a maximum, in order to encourage persons and partnerships to engage in formal economic activities and to establish new projects.

TAXES AND DUTIES ON BUILDINGS

The tax on income from buildings was imposed by Law 56 of 1954, which has been amended so often and affected by so many supplementary laws that legislation regulating real estate taxes and duties has become too complicated even for specialists; it overflows with contradictions and discrepancies.

First, there are housing units that are exempt from all real estate taxes, both original and additional, while there are other units that are exempt from the original tax only and not from the additional taxes and duties. Further, there is a third category of units that are subject to all real estate taxes and duties, both original and additional, the total of which may reach a rate of 44 percent of their total rental value or 55.5 percent of their net rental value, the burden of which falls entirely upon the owner if he is the occupant of the unit.

Second, there are units or buildings (such as those which are not subject to rental control and which are occupied by the owners themselves, among which are factory buildings) whose real estate taxes and duties escalate in huge steps when their rental values are reassessed every ten years, thus reaching five or ten times the previous assessment. On the other hand, there are other units or buildings whose real estate taxes and duties do not change substantially when reassessment is made every ten years (such as the units whose rents are fixed by law).

Third, Law 136 of 1981 which went into effect on January 1, 1982, exempted buildings constructed in 1977 and onward from all original and additional real estate taxes as long as they are below the 'luxurious standard.' Buildings of luxurious standard, on the other hand, are subjected to all real estate taxes and duties, the rate of which could reach 44 percent of the total rental value as stated above.

Fourth, there are real estate duties imposed on the total rental value, and there are other real estate taxes and duties imposed on the net rental value (that is after deducting 20 percent thereof). Also there is the minute differentiation between what constitutes a real estate tax and what is considered a real estate duty. While the real estate taxes enjoy exemptions provided for by law, real estate duties do not enjoy these exemptions.

Fifth, while buildings that are used for purposes other than residence are subject to the original tax rate of 10 percent, units that were originally assigned for residence but are used for other purposes are subject to the original real estate tax at its progressive rate which could reach 40 percent.

The government, in realization of the shortcomings listed above, attempted to rectify them through Law 187 of 1993 amending Income Tax Law 157 of 1981. According to this amendment, the rental value of the building or housing unit is included in the income subject to the unified personal income tax, and then the original real estate tax is deducted from the unified tax due, on condition that the deduction should not exceed the amount of the real estate tax. Nevertheless, this correction does not cover all cases or kinds of taxpayers. Furthermore, any reform should essentially stem from the legislation regulating the real estate taxes and duties. Therefore, new legislation should be issued to regulate taxes and duties on buildings in a comprehensive way, and it should be characterized by simplicity, clarity, and coherence to avoid the contradictions in the present legislation. However, to realize equity in the area of real estate taxes and duties, a new law regulating the relationship between landlords and tenants should be issued to determine, among other things, the equitable rental amount on the basis of which the real estate taxes and duties will be assessed.

The 20 percent that is deducted from the rental value, in consideration of all expenses and maintenance, no longer represents a sufficient or fair percentage in most cases. In fact, in many buildings the rate of expenses and maintenance reaches 50 percent or more of the total rental value. At the same time, the original real estate tax rate on units with an average rent per room exceeding LE10 is 40 percent, which is a very high rate considering that none of the buildings constructed now have an average rent per room as low as LE10. The rate designated for expenses and maintenance should be raised to 30 percent or 40 percent, and the progressive tax rate structure should be reviewed to be less burdensome and more realistic.

TAXES ON GAINS FROM THE SALE OF SECURITIES

Article 11 of Law 95 of 1992, relating to the Capital Market, stipulates that when shares are sold for an amount greater than their purchase price, the increase is subject to a tax at the rate of 2 percent to be borne by the seller. Also article 14 of the same law provides for the application of the 2 percent tax to gains from the sale of bonds, debentures, and other similar securities.

Because articles 11 and 14 of Law 95 did not exempt companies and other legal entities subject to the corporate tax, and commercial and industrial enterprises subject to the unified tax, from the 2 percent tax, gains from the sale of securities made by such companies and enterprises will be subject to the 2 percent tax and then again to the corporate tax or the unified tax as the case may be. It is likely that the legislature did not intend to punish the said companies and enterprises by subjecting their gains from the sale of securities twice to taxes, since there is no justification whatsoever for this. On the contrary, the state is keen to encourage investment and to revive the stock exchange. Law 95 of 1992 should be amended to exempt companies and enterprises that are subject to the corporate tax, and commercial and industrial enterprises that are subject to the unified tax, from the 2 percent tax on gains from the sale of securities.

Also, it is worth noting that the 2 percent tax on the sale of securities is applied at present only to securities that are registered in the official lists of the stock exchange. It is difficult to find any justification for such discrimination, especially since the tax exemptions prescribed for the securities registered in these official lists decreased when the general income tax was canceled and will possibly be removed altogether in the near future.

THE GENERAL SALES TAX

The general tax on sales was imposed by Law 11 of 1991, which came into force as of May 3, 1991. The general tax on sales is a form of indirect tax, just like the customs taxes, which will ultimately be borne by the consumer.

The standard rate of the sales tax is 10 percent of the value of all industrial commodities whether produced locally or imported. The law also imposed a sales tax on some services as listed in schedule 2 attached thereto and whose rate varies between 5 percent and 10 percent. Presidential Decree 180 of 1991, effective May 4, 1991, exempted certain essential commodities from the sales tax and introduced three categories of rates besides the standard rate for commodities: a reduced rate, to be set at 5 percent on some foodstuffs and touristic services; a medium rate, to be set at 20 percent on some durable goods; and a high rate, to be set at 30 percent on luxury goods.

Presidential Decree 180 of 1991 was amended by Presidential Decree 295 of 1993, effective July 29, 1993, to unify the two rates of 20 percent and 30 percent in a single rate of 25 percent. For some social and fiscal considerations, the legislature decided to keep a limited number of commodities subject to the rates of the repealed consumption tax law. These commodities are listed in schedule 1 attached to the law.

From the aforementioned, it is apparent that the rate of the sales tax is not uniform for all commodities. Although this causes some complications in determining the appropriate tax rate to be applied, it gives a degree of fairness that is usually lacking in indirect taxes. Presented below are the major problems and deficiencies found in the sales tax law and its implementation, as well as recommendations for remedying these problems.

Sales tax on capital equipment. According to the sales tax law, the sales tax is imposed on all industrial commodities, whether locally produced or imported, except for those with special exemptions. Therefore, capital machinery and equipment are subject to the sales tax, in spite of the fact that they are for use in production and are not for sale. Since this tax cannot be deducted from the sales tax collected on sales, the production costs are increased by the amount of this tax and, subsequently, the prices of the goods produced. This discourages investment. This tax situation is not found in advanced or developing countries such as the United Kingdom, France, Indonesia, and Malaysia. The sales tax on capital equipment should be revised either by removing it altogether or by allowing for the deduction of this tax from the total sales tax collected on the products of the project when they are sold.

Sales tax on imports and 'first sale'. Article 11 of the sales tax law stipulates that, for the purpose of computing the sales tax, the value of the imported commodity is deemed to be the total of the value used in the determination of customs taxes plus the said customs taxes and other applicable taxes and duties.

In many cases, the customs authorities do not acknowledge the value of the commodity as stated in the source invoice, but estimate a higher value, thus causing an increase in both customs taxes and the sales tax. When the importer determines the selling price of his commodity (for the 'first sale,' as it is termed), he takes into consideration the actual import cost of the commodity and the customs taxes paid and adds a reasonable margin of profit to arrive at his selling price on the basis of which he collects the sales tax from the buyer.

Usually, the Sales Tax Authority disregards the actual selling price determined by the importer in the aforementioned manner, then estimates a higher price for the first sale commensurate with the price increase made by customs officials, and, on the basis of this estimate, assesses the sales tax. This leads to discrepancies between the sales tax as assessed by the Sales Tax Authority and the actual sales tax collected by the importer. As a result of this practice, the importer bears the unexpected difference in the sales tax and, instead of being an intermediary in collecting the sales tax, he actually pays part of the sales tax himself.

The sales tax on imported goods should be determined when the commodity is released from customs on the basis of the price stated in the exporter's invoice, and the sales tax on the first sale should be determined on the basis of the first sale invoice as issued by the importer without any adjustment, unless there is strong evidence that his invoice has been falsified. Finally, should the sales tax collected by the importer in the month of accounting prove to be less than the sales tax paid by him on clearing the commodity, the importer should have the right to deduct the difference from the sales tax collections of the following month.

Sales tax on 'aftersale-service'. In many cases, and especially in cases where importers sell machinery or equipment, the sale contract includes a guarantee or warranty period during which the seller (importer) will provide spare parts and repair the machinery or equipment, in case of any defect, free of any charge; this is called aftersale services. Since the importer does not receive payment for the spare parts replaced during the guarantee period, he does not collect sales tax thereon. However, the Sales Tax Authority insists that the importer should issue a selling invoice for the spare parts provided and the maintenance made during the guarantee period and thus should collect sales tax. Obviously this is not the case, since the importer, when fixing the selling price of the machinery or equipment, has included in the price the estimated cost of spare parts and maintenance during the guarantee period, and the sales tax collected on his first sale covers, inter alia, the cost of these spare parts and maintenance.

Given that the guarantee period and aftersale service is a worldwide system that cannot be changed, the Sales Tax Authority should respect this system and refrain from collecting sales tax on spare parts and maintenance provided during the guarantee period because the sales tax thereon has been already collected at the first sale.

Sales tax on processing for others. Presidential Decree 77 of 1992 added new services to schedule 2 attached to the law listing services which are subject to the sales tax at the rate of 10 percent. Among these services is "processing for others." Presidential Decree 77 of 1992 did not, however, define what constitutes "processing for others" and the minister of finance did not issue any definition, nor did he specify the details of services that come under "processing for others." The Sales Tax Authority issued Circular 41 of 1992, dated June 4, 1992, specifying the conditions under which a service could be defined as a "processing for others." These conditions are: the processing must be performed on a certain commodity or material; the commodity must be owned by someone other than the person performing the processing; the outcome of processing is to transfer the material (commodity) into a new product as deemed by law; and the fees collected by the provider of the "processing for others" should be LE54,000 or more per year.

On April 18, 1993, the Sales Tax Authority issued Instruction 3 of 1993 expanding the scope of services that come under "processing for others" to include the following: services of repair, maintenance, installation, contracting, and transportation. Although Circular 41 of 1992 gave a logical definition of what constitutes processing for others, Instruction 3 of 1993 lacked any logic in the specific services which it included under this category. If we were to follow the line of this instruction, then any service could come under "processing for others."

Instruction 3 of 1993 caused many disputes between the Sales Tax Authority and the contracting and transportation companies because these companies considered Instruction 3 of 1993 to be illogical and not supported by law. In addition to this, the implementation of Instruction 3 of 1993 caused a tremendous increase in the value of the invoices of the contracting and transportation companies to the extent that their customers refused to pay, even though a large portion of these customers were governmental bodies. As a way out of this dilemma, the Sales Tax Authority resorted to the Egyptian Federation of Building and Construction Contractors in order to persuade the contractors to apply the sales tax on contracting works.

The repeal of the sales tax on contracting works, transportation, repair, maintenance, and installation services as stated in Instruction 3 of 1993 is recommended for three reasons: first, transportation has nothing to do with commodities owned by others; second, contract works do not result in an industrial commodity according to the technical definition of the word; and third, repair, maintenance, and installation services do not transfer material into a new industrial commodity. Additionally, no definition was given to the "processing for others" by the appropriate authority such that this definition, with the types of services that come under it, can be published in Egypt's Official Gazette and be known and binding to all those concerned.

THE FISCAL STAMP TAX

The fiscal stamp tax is imposed at present by virtue of Law 111 of 1980, which replaced Law 224 of 1951. During the last seven years, the specific stamp tax rates have increased by 400 percent, and the proportional stamp tax rates have increased by 200 percent, so that stamp taxes have become equally onerous for the ordinary citizen, for the businessman, and for the investor. A quick glance at the stamp tax rates on some transactions and documents will clarify this:

On shares, debentures, and the capitals of companies in general: 1.2 percent annually;

On the sale / purchase of shares and debentures: 0.4 percent (shared equally between the seller and purchaser);

On governmental payments in consideration of services and supplies: about 2.4 percent on each payment;

On credits: 1 percent annually (shared equally between the bank and customer);

On loans and debts: 0.8 percent;

On life insurance premiums: 3 percent;

On general insurance premiums: 15–20 percent;

On the total insurance premiums collected by insurance companies: 0.8 percent annually;

On advertising in newspapers, magazines, cinemas, and TV: 36 percent of the publication or projection charge.

If we compare some of these rates with the rates applied by some advanced or developed countries, the following is discovered: in the U.K., the stamp duty on general insurance premiums is imposed at the rate of 3 percent, and no stamp duty is levied on life insurance premiums. The stamp tax on the transfer of ownership of shares is 3 percent without imposing a stamp duty on the share capital of companies. In France, the stamp tax is imposed at 4.8 percent on the transfer of ownership of shares, but there is no stamp tax on the share capital of companies. In Indonesia, the stamp tax rates vary in general between 0.05 percent and 0.1 percent. While in Malaysia the stamp tax on the transfer of ownership of shares is 0.3 percent, without imposing a stamp tax on the share capital of companies. In general, the types of fiscal stamp taxes applied in Egypt do not have counterparts in these countries; also, the stamp tax rates applied in these countries are much lower than the corresponding rates in Egypt.

Since the fiscal stamp tax is imposed on documents and transactions without consideration of the varying contributory capacities of those paying the stamp taxes, any increase in the rates of this tax places heavy and unfair burden on the less affluent. It also contributes to a rise in the prices of commodities and services which in turn negatively affects investment and business trends. In order to encourage investment and savings, the fiscal stamp tax on shares, debentures, and capital of companies in general should be canceled. And in order to encourage insurance, the stamp tax on life insurance should be canceled and that on general insurance should be greatly reduced. In other words, the fiscal stamp tax law needs a comprehensive revision.

The previous Fiscal Stamp Duty Law 224 of 1951 stated in article 6, chapter 2, that the fiscal stamp duty may be collected only once on any banking transaction, if such a transaction assumes several forms, and shall be based on the higher duty. This provision was to avoid any kind of double taxation. When the Fiscal Stamp Tax Law 111 of 1981 was issued, this important provision was dropped or ignored, and consequently the proportional stamp tax is now levied, for example, on the loan contract at a rate of 0.8 percent and then on the promissory note, processed in execution thereto, at a rate of 0.6 percent, which constitutes a double taxation on the same banking transaction.

This situation leads to doubling the already high burden of stamp taxes on banking transactions. The negative effect of this double taxation is increased by the fact that most banking transactions are of large amounts. The present fiscal stamp tax law should be amended by the addition of a provision prohibiting the imposition of the stamp tax on any banking transaction more than once, if such a transaction assumes more than one form.

Article 83 of the stamp tax law also imposes an annual stamp tax on debentures, shares, or quotas issued by joint-stock companies, partnerships limited by shares, limited liability companies, and on the designated capital of branches of foreign companies at a rate of 1.2

percent of the nominal value. If the shares of such companies are traded on the stock exchange, the tax is imposed annually at a rate of 0.8 percent of their market value. At the same time, the fiscal stamp tax is imposed on the selling and purchasing of securities at the rate of 0.4 percent to be borne equally by both the seller and the purchaser with a maximum amount of LE24 each. The imposition of this stamp tax on the capital of companies in general is, in fact, a confiscation of a part of the invested capital—something rejected by the investor, causing him to recalculate his options before proceeding with a new investment or increasing the capital of the company in which he is an investor. Furthermore, the said stamp tax is imposed on the capital of companies, even those sustaining losses, and thereby has a double negative effect. Except for the motive of levying, this tax serves no useful economic or social purposes. There is no similar stamp tax levied in advanced countries or developing countries. The proportional stamp tax on shares, debentures, and the capital of companies in general should be repealed.

Article 57 of the stamp tax law also imposes a stamp tax on the contracts and operations of granting credits (on the portion thereof which is uncovered by cash) at the rate of 1 percent. The tax is borne equally between the party granting the credit and the party receiving the credit. If the period of the credit contract or operation, or its renewal, exceeds one year, the stamp tax is reimposed for each additional year or fraction of a year. The legal jurists defined the credit as a promise by a bank to its customer to place at his disposal a definite sum of money for a specific period of time, during which the customer shall be entitled to withdraw all or part of the sum. In spite of this definition, the tax administration has expanded on the credit concept and has started to apply it to all forms of financial facilities granted by banks, such as the issuance of letters of guarantee, the discounting of bills of exchange and promissory notes, and the opening of letters of credit for importing goods, and so on.

This expansion in the credit concept has led to disputes between taxpayers and the tax administration, many of which have been referred to the courts of law. It should be noted, in this regard, that the tax administration itself does not follow one rule in assessing the tax on credits, as the tax treatment varies from one case to the other and from one tax inspector to another according to the concept of credit adopted thereby. Although the rulings of the courts in the majority of cases accept the more strict definition of credit, as indicated above, recently a few court rulings have been issued which upheld the Tax Authority's expanded concept.

In addition to the foregoing, the application of article 57, which requires that the stamp tax be levied on credit contracts and operations, leads to a repetition in the imposition of the credit stamp tax: once on the total credit contract or agreement, and a second time on each credit transaction arising from the credit contract. This situation has led to the accumulation of disputes between taxpayers and the tax administration and to a certain instability in the tax position of the taxpayers, most of whom are banks. Furthermore, considering that half the proportional stamp tax on credits is borne by the banks' customers for whom credits are opened, banks face a problem in determining the exact burden of the proportional stamp tax that should be collected from their customers. In most cases, the bank will decide to charge its customers with the amount calculated in accordance with the strict definition of the credit and thus will have to bear any extra stamp differences resulting from the final assessment made later on by the Tax Authority, which are usually very substantial.

In view of all of the above, canceling the proportional stamp tax on credits and replacing it with the stamp tax on loans and debts may be advisable. This will not alter the tax proceeds significantly since any real credit will end in a loan or debt. However, should the government see fit to retain the stamp tax on credits, then it shall be necessary to formulate an accurate legal definition of a credit, and the double taxation resulting from imposing the stamp tax on both the overall credit contract and each of its withdrawal operations should be avoided. Accordingly, the relevant internal instructions to this effect should be issued by the tax administration and should be binding for all tax inspectors.

Finally, there exists a delay in examining and assessing the fiscal stamp tax by the tax administration which ranges between three to five years. Such delay, in addition to the disputes concerning the assessment of this tax (such as the dispute concerning the concept of the credit referred to earlier), increases the negative effects from which the major payers of this tax (such as banks) suffer, in that their tax positions are insecure, and that they are unable to claim from their customers the refund of their share in any additional stamp tax differences resulting from the final assessment. The delay in the tax inspection and assessment is, however, a general phenomenon which would require improving the overall efficiency of the tax administration.

THE INHERITANCE TAX

The inheritance tax was imposed by Law 228 of 1989, which replaced Law 142 of 1944, while Law 195 of 1952, which imposed a tax on estates, was abolished. This inheritance tax is imposed on the share of each heir in the estate of the deceased person. It applies to all real estate and movable property existing in Egypt or abroad if the deceased was an Egyptian, whether he was resident in Egypt or abroad; on all the real estate property existing in Egypt if the deceased was a foreigner, irrespective of his place of residence; and on all the real estate and movable property existing in Egypt if the deceased was a foreigner resident in Egypt.

Law 228 of 1989 reduced the tax burden on heirs to a great extent as compared with the tax burden under Laws 142 of 1944 and 195 of 1952; nevertheless, several intractable problems remain. First, the official papers and documents required to be submitted by the heirs to enable release of the estate are the same as those papers and documents that were required under the repealed laws. Issuing and obtaining these documents require great time and effort. Second, the proceeds to the State Treasury from this tax did not exceed an amount of LE7.5 million in fiscal year 1993/94. If we take into consideration the costs incurred to collect this revenue, we will find that they far exceed the actual gains. Finally, most countries, whether advanced or developing, do not impose this tax. In light of these points, this tax should be completely abolished.

Seven

Financing Private Sector Development in Egypt

The American Chamber of Commerce in Egypt

Egypt is now faced with the challenging task of restructuring its productive sector (both state and privately owned), expanding private ownership, and achieving rapid real growth in private investment. Superior saving performance, higher mobility of financial resources, and greater access by the private sector to these resources will need to be the essential features of the financial framework that will enable the private sector to tackle these challenges. Three elements comprise this framework: the available sources of finance, the institutional intermediaries operative in the financial sector, and the instruments that are used by these institutions to mobilize financial resources and channel them to investors.

The efficiency of financial sector operators in mobilizing and allocating resources is very sensitive to the government's fiscal and monetary policies. Over the last three years, the management of foreign exchange and money markets through treasury bills proved to be a successful policy during a period of aggregate demand-side reform. Today, in a quest for a market-driven, private-sector-led economy, supply-side reforms call for new financial sector policies and regulations that would lower interest rates, improve saving performance, facilitate capital mobility, and boost investment.

This chapter focuses on the current state of Egypt's financial sector in terms of saving performance, the capacity of intermediaries to mobilize and channel those savings, and the adequacy of the instruments available to these intermediaries. It also touches on the taxation policies that affect the performance of the operators in the financial sector. For each element, the major constraints are discussed. Finally, a list of suggestions as to what should be included in a financial sector reform agenda with a view to private sector development (PSD) is offered.

AVAILABLE FINANCIAL RESOURCES

For the purpose of immediate-term PSD, Egypt's saving performance may be acceptable. In the long run, however, this saving performance will have to make major leaps in order to sustain the levels of investment needed over the next decade. Egypt's gross domestic saving as a percentage of gross domestic product (GDP) averaged 9 percent between 1980 and 1990. If these savings are channeled properly and structural adjustments are successful in increasing the allocative efficiency of the Egyptian economy, Egypt may well be on its way to a sustainable cycle of saving and investment. However, consider the magnitude of the improvement needed—gross domestic savings as a percentage of GDP over the past decade, on average, was less than half of that of Argentina, one quarter that of Mexico, and one fifth that of Malaysia or Thailand.

One important feature stands out in Egypt's domestic saving pattern: the bank deposits of private enterprises are low in relation to their bank credit. Over the past five years, the average ratio of deposits made by private enterprises to the credit drawn by them was 1:2. This ratio is even higher for proprietorships and simple partnerships, which constitute over three-quarters of private establishments and account for one-third and more than one-half of private enterprises' deposits and credits, respectively.

In Egypt, the tax treatment of noncorporate firms does not allow these firms to retain reserves before distribution of profits to their owners. A noncorporate firm is subject to a tax on commercial and industrial profits identical to that on incorporated firms. But the definition of taxable income is not quite the same for noncorporate and corporate firms. The profits and interest payments of these businesses, net of the commercial and industrial profits tax and the tax on movable capital, are then taxed under the general income tax. In combination, this implies a combined tax rate that can be as high as 76 percent. More critically, individuals can deduct the funds they spend buying corporate debt and equity, but not the funds they spend investing in noncorporate firms. This tax treatment limits the saving capacity of noncorporate firms. Since most firms in Egypt start and continue to operate as simple partnerships or proprietorships, the net impact is a low saving performance of private enterprises at large.

The second important feature of the domestic saving pattern in Egypt is the high share of bank deposits in total household savings as compared to contractual savings pools like insurance, pensions, and social security. The problem lies in the costs and benefits of the social

Table 7-1
Stocks of deposits in domestic banks by source, 1993 (LE millions)

	Type of deposit			
	Current	Term	Blocked	Total
Public enterprise	6,009	8,676	4,426	19,111
Private enterprise	3,990	7,612	2,432	14,034
Government	16,583	27,182	747	44,512
Households	4,888	67,760	1,194	73,842
Others	1,760	6,918	138	8,816
Insurance and pension	54	776	0	830
Social insurance	9	734	3	746
Bank Nasser	112	239	0	351
Insurance companies	71	1,795	195	2,061
National Investment Bank	2,205	461	0	2,666
Total	35,681	122,153	9,135	166,969

Source: CAPMAS

Table 7-2
Net household savings during FY 1991–92

Saving pool	(LE millions)	Percentage of total
Banks pool		
Deposits	9,040,544	45.85
Savings accounts	1,399,637	7.1
Saving certificates	3,545,465	18
Investment certificates	915,858	4.65
Total in banks	14,901,504	75.6
Post office savings	39,253	0.2
Social insurance	2,089,778	10.6
Insurance and pensions	2,554,501	13
Life and general insurance	131,784	0.6
Total savings	19,716,820	100

Source: CAPMAS

security schemes and the shallowness of both the general and life insurance markets. Recent studies of the social security system in Egypt illustrate that contribution rates for social security are kept extraordinarily high (41 percent of basic wage, with employer carrying 26 percent) to compensate for low returns on assets, and that a public sector and civil service employee receives higher pension benefits than a private sector employee. It is no surprise then that the portion of private sector nonagricultural employees covered by social security in Egypt does not exceed 30 percent. In effect, the social security system—an important source of contractual saving in Egypt—is tapping a very small base of its potential market.

FINANCIAL INTERMEDIARY INSTITUTIONS

Banks, a securities market, insurance firms (general and life insurance), pension funds, and the social security system are the key financial intermediary institutions that mobilize savings and channel them to investment. In Egypt, private sector access to the financial resources of these institutions is very limited. An array of policies and regulations that both inhibit the growth and efficiency of these institutions and administratively allocate their resources militate against their use as a source of capital for private investment.

Ideally, financial sector regulations should ensure that intermediary institutions are competitive. Entry and exit should be easy and not excessively costly. The threat of potential competition should prevent existing institutions from developing anticompetitive practices; a level playing field should be created for all market participants; individual institutions should enjoy considerable managerial autonomy and make decisions based on economic criteria; and an effective set of prudential regulations should be urged to discourage imprudent and fraudulent behavior.

Banks

The banking sector suffers from a very high degree of concentration; its industrial structure approaches an oligopoly. Product diversification (long-term finance, small business lending, consumer credit, etc.) is limited, pricing is not yet completely competitive, and the market is segmented. These features are a result of high barriers to entry, prudential regulations that are unjustifiably restrictive especially for branches of foreign banks, reserve and liquidity requirements that inflate the cost of funds for all banks, and a government fiscal policy that discourages banks from taking private sector lending risks. Add to that Egypt's legal and judiciary systems, which reportedly cause uncertainty regarding debt recovery, accentuate the risk of doing business, and inflate transaction costs for banks and other businesses alike.

The Egyptian banking system consists of ninety-eight banks: four public sector commercial banks; forty private and joint venture commercial banks; eleven 'investment' banks; twenty-two foreign bank branches; and twenty-one specialized banks (two real estate, one industrial, and eighteen agricultural banks). Many of the investment banks are joint ventures between public sector banks and international banks. Private commercial banks and investment banks were initially chartered under different laws, but currently there is little difference in their business mix and operations.

The four large public sector banks alone account for 55 percent of total bank assets. Other commercial banks have 22 percent, and business and investment banks have 16 percent. The remaining 7 percent is held by the specialized banks. The level of concentration becomes apparent when the public sector banks' shares in the joint venture banks is taken into account. This makes them holders of over 90 percent of the total assets of commercial banks. The dominance of purely public sector institutions is heightened even further if the National Investment Bank (NIB) is also taken into account. The NIB holds exclusive rights to the vast long-term resources mobilized by the social security system estimated at LE24 billion, equivalent to 25 percent of total bank deposits in 1992.

Regulatory barriers to competition include administrative restrictions on the licensing of domestic banks, restrictions on branching, restrictions on foreign bank entry, and restrictions on the types of activities that banks are allowed to undertake. The Central Bank of Egypt (CBE) requires a minimum authorized capital for new banks of LE100 million, of which LE50 million must be fully paid up (that is, US$30 million and US$15 million respectively). Banks are also barred from extending to a single client credit facilities of any kind exceeding 25 percent of their paid-in capital and reserves. This rule applies to foreign branches regardless of the financial health of the parent bank, effectively underutilizing the capacity of multinational banks to fund large-scale projects. These relatively demanding regulations have recently dissuaded several foreign banks from entering the Egyptian market.

Reserve and liquidity requirements are imposed on both local and foreign currency deposits. Banks have to observe a reserve ratio of 15 percent on local currency deposits in the form of non-interest-bearing reserve balances with the CBE, as well as an additional liquidity ratio of 20 percent, which can be in the form of excess reserve balances, net interbank deposits, treasury bills, or commercial bills. For foreign currency deposits, the reserve and liquidity ratios are 15 percent and 25 percent, respectively, both in the form of interest-bearing accounts. These two ratios clearly operate as a tax on bank intermediation which raises the cost of funds.

The deregulation of interest rates in 1992 represented the removal of an important layer of banking regulations. However, banks—

especially state-owned ones—are still not competitive in pricing their services. Detailed tariff schedules and guidelines for most banking services are issued by the Egyptian Bankers Association and endorsed by the CBE. In fact, much of the reaction by the Egyptian banking system to the deregulation of interest rates appears to have followed a pattern that is found in other countries which undertook similar financial sector reforms. The selective impact in favor of large public sector banks; the rise in banks' liquidity; the attempt to coordinate interest rates and pricing of services; the growing concern about nonperforming loans; the need to modernize banking practices; and the desire for financial innovation, all have been observed in Indonesia, Sri Lanka, Turkey, Tunisia, Hungary, Mexico, and Chile.

Retail business is dominated by the large public sector banks, which enjoy relatively large branch networks—on average two hundred branches each—and are, consequently, able to raise most of the retail deposits. The product mix of most of the other banks is tilted toward wholesale business and upscale customers. The joint venture banks specialize in providing short-term working capital and trade finance. They are particularly active in the market for large- and middle-scale private sector companies and, occasionally, public sector companies for trade-related financial services. The local branches of foreign banks increasingly focus on fee-based services that include, among other things, trade-related financial services, advice on mergers, and active participation in debt-to-equity swaps.

Another very important feature of the banking sector in Egypt is the severe shortage of long-term credit, especially for the private sector. While three-quarters of the credit extended by the domestic commercial, investment, and specialized banks is short term (one year or less), historically the government and the state-owned enterprises enjoyed monopoly access to long-term finance provided by the NIB and international funding agencies and donors—a situation which resulted from the past policy of administering credit and allocating priority quotas for public sector firms. This system was dismantled as part of Egypt's economic reform and structural adjustment program; but the symptoms still persist. There are no conclusive analyses as to why the banking sector has not as yet been prompted to offer long-term credit to the private sector. Some experts point to a number of reasons which vary from the lack of access to the types of savings that would allow longer-term matching maturities (a problem which could be remedied if banks are allowed to bid freely for the social security funds or other long-term sources); the weak state of contract enforcement institutions, which heightens risks for

Table 7-3
Term structure of credit extended by Egypt's investment and commercial banks (percentage of total for the year)

	One year or less		Over one year		Overdue	
	1990	1993	1990	1993	1990	1993
Investment banks	6	7	7	6	7	4
Commercial banks	68	74	9	9	3	0
Total	74	81	16	15	10	4

Source: calculated from CBE annual reports

Table 7-4
Term structure of credit extended by Egyptian banks, 1993 (percentage)

	One year or less	Over one year	Total
Public Sector Banks	61	10	71
Private Sector Banks	22	7	29
Total	83	17	100

Source: calculated from 1994 CAPMAS figures

long-term lending; the problematic securitization regulations; or the lack of competitive pressure on banks, while others advocate that it is a case of market failure.

Securities market

During the past five years, on average, less than 5 percent of the capital raised by both the public and private firms combined came from the securities market. Historically, the public sector, which dominated the economy, generated very little demand for securities because it relied on public sector financial institutions for its funding. Today, the Egyptian government's privatization strategy rests, inter alia, on the sale of public enterprise shares in the stock exchange. The People's Assembly passed the new Capital Market Law 95 of 1992, which introduces important improvements and paves the way for both privatization through public offerings and greater access by the private sector to capital raised in the securities market. There remains, however, some impediments to the takeoff of this market.

First, the services offered by the existing stock exchanges are not well developed, trading settlement is slow, financial information is very scarce and when found is of little use to investors. The stock exchanges in Cairo and Alexandria operate under the Stock Exchange Law 161 of 1957, as amended in 1959 and 1981, and are governed by the Ministry of Economy. These two exchanges are viable only because listing fees are artificially inflated by the requirement that all joint-stock companies must apply for listing on both exchanges within three years of profitable operation. Further protection of the existing exchanges is also provided in the new Capital Market Law (CML). While this law provides for the establishment of new stock exchanges with a minimum capital requirement of LE10 million, it does not allow the listing of stocks in more than one exchange and exempts the Cairo and Alexandria stock exchanges from this provision. Closed joint-stock companies are also encouraged by the tax benefits of listing. The CML continues to extend tax benefits for closed joint-stock companies, although they serve no market development purpose. The existing stock exchanges should be exposed to greater competitive pressure.

Second, the portfolio management practices of institutional investors (pension funds, insurance companies, etc.) contribute to the lack of market liquidity. Even today, with the relatively small volume of trading, institutional trading reportedly accounts for about 90 percent of average daily volume. Several restrictions are placed on the portfolios of these institutions by their governing bodies. This issue is discussed further below.

Insurance, pension funds, and social insurance programs

Contractual savings (CS) can cause a shift in favor of long-term financial resources that could be used to promote the development of corporate equity and bond markets. Corporate equities, as well as longer-term debt securities, can be developed to complement the short-term instruments available in the local banking and money markets. By investing in stocks, corporate bonds, and long-term government bonds, CS could change wealth composition in favor of financial assets that can be intermediated locally to expand the supply of reproductive capital. CS may also play an important role in managing domestic public debt by increasing the demand for long-term government bonds. This is important, especially since the maturity of newly issued public debt in Egypt is limited to short-term treasury bills.

The insurance sector's contribution to Egypt's GDP is around 1 percent, a low level when compared to 2 percent in the Philippines and Thailand or 3 percent in Cyprus and Chile. In Egypt, as in most developing countries, the insurance industry is underdeveloped, the level of income and wealth of the large majority of the Egyptian people is still quite low, and reliance on informal insurance arrangements is strong. There are reasons to believe, however, that there are financial resources in the market which could be tapped if the insurance sector were liberalized.

The regulatory framework governing insurance companies impedes the development of this industry, which is characterized by high concentration and limited product innovation. The Egyptian Insurance Supervisory Authority (EISA) fixes rates, brokerage commissions, and reinsurance discounts. Although the number of state-owned companies and private companies appears to be balanced (four state-owned companies versus five private ones), the large majority of the insurance business is controlled by the state-owned companies. In terms of annual gross premia, 85 percent of the total is managed by the state-owned direct insurers. Participation by foreign capital is forbidden in local insurance companies operating in the domestic market. Direct foreign ownership is allowed only for companies operating in the free zones.

Entry barriers are high not due to high equity requirements nor to the complexity of the procedures for setting up a new company; but, instead, barriers are created by EISA's power to decide whether or not there is room in the market for a new insurance company to enter the insurance sector. Such power, given under Law 10, allows it to deny entry into the market, without legal recourse.

There are two schemes for private pension funds in Egypt: Private Complementary Pension Funds (PCPFs) and Private Alternative Pension Funds (PAPFs). The most serious constraint on both types of funds is the tight control exercised by EISA on the allocation of their financial resources (see financial instruments diversification below).

PCPFs are regulated by Law 54 of 1975 and its Executive Regulation (Decree 78 of 1977). They can be formed without initial capital by people grouped in a union, organization, profession, company, and so forth, to provide its members with work disability and other retirement benefits. A PCPF must be registered with EISA before it starts operating; it must submit to that authority a contributions and benefits plan, as well as a list of its bylaws. Every five years each PCPF must present for endorsement a financial statement made by an actuary registered with EISA.

PAPFs operate under Law 64 of 1980 and its Executive Decree 52 of 1985. PAPFs receive contributions from members, employers, and the state social insurance systems for those members who opt for substituting the state's system for their PAPF. The funds belong to the members and are managed by a self-appointed board of directors. The sponsoring company where the members work also participates on the board of directors and names the chairman of the fund.

A PAPF must be registered under the Ministry of Social Insurance, which controls its performance. To register, the PAPF must also submit its bylaws and financial and actuary projections (certified by a registered actuary), have over one thousand members, and have paid-up capital of over LE10 million (around $3 million). Currently, there is a total of eight PAPFs operating with reserve funds totaling LE116 million and $15 million. Due to problems in the governing law, PAPFs have not grown as fast as the PCPFs. Seven out of the eight PAPFs are linked to banks.

The Social Insurance (SI) programs that cover public and private employees in the formal sector are more than adequately funded. The contribution rates are high, current benefit payouts are relatively low, and the operating surplus is healthy. The fiscal position of the large social insurance programs is reasonably secure over the short and medium terms. The major problem for the SI programs is the investment of their surpluses. All operating SI surpluses are deposited in the NIB where they are credited with very low nominal rates of return. Historically, interest rates were as low as 5 percent as compared to the 13 percent (still a negative real rate of return at that time) which was offered by commercial banks. Subsequently, the NIB raised the rate on new deposits to 6 percent, then 8 percent, and finally to 11 percent in 1991. These raises applied only to new deposits; old deposits are still earning the extraordinarily low rates.

Inflation has substantially eroded the real value of the SI reserves. According to recent estimates, if the General Authority for Social Insurance (GASI) reserve has earned a zero real return on its NIB-held funds (rather than a negative real return), the asset holdings in the reserve would have been worth more than twice as much at the end of 1990/91 (LE44 billion rather than LE21 billion). Even if GASI had received no transfers from the Treasury during the 1980s, the reserve would still have held nearly 50 percent more assets at the end of 1990/91 (LE30 billion versus LE21 billion). It is clear that the SI funds provided a substantial net subsidy to the NIB and the state, while none of these funds have been accessed by the private sector.

Mutual funds and portfolio management firms

Mutual funds do not, as of yet, play the desired role of providing investors with the opportunity to diversify their holdings. The new capital market law introduced several provisions that will enable mutual funds and fund management companies to assume a proactive role in savings mobilizations and investments. A healthy diversity of venture capital funds, underwriters, and brokerage and custodial services firms are contemplated in the new law. Investments made through mutual funds are also treated favorably by the Egyptian tax code. But there remains several regulatory issues that may impair the operations of mutual funds and fund management companies.

First, the process of entry seems to be a painstaking one, with excessive administrative controls. Conditions for establishing mutual funds and fund management companies are spelled out in the CML and its executive regulations, but the licensing of those applicants who meet such conditions is not automatic. Like in the case of insurance companies, the Capital Market Authority (CMA) applies very subjective criteria to grant or deny licenses. The rules of entry are also not yet clearly laid out. Tests that are administered by the CMA to verify the management qualifications of new applicants are not transparent and the criteria for reserve requirements are not yet defined.

Second, prudential regulations are heavily biased in favor of bank sponsored funds in comparison to those that are privately established by individuals or nonbanking institutions. The leveraging ratio allowed for bank-owned funds is 1:20 versus 1:10 for private nonbank funds. Mutual funds established by banks are also allowed to issue multiple funds while others are allowed only one. Furthermore, the establishment of open-ended funds are allowed exclusively for banks. Private nonbank funds cannot make new issues to replace those that are redeemed by their owners.

Third, fund management firms managing mutual funds are favored over those managing portfolios. It is not clear why the minimum capital requirement for mutual fund management companies is LE1 million, while that for portfolio management is LE3 million.

FINANCIAL INSTRUMENTS DIVERSIFICATION

Banks' lending activities are severely hampered by the provisions of Egypt's outdated civil and commercial codes which date back to 1883 and 1984, respectively. The lack of a system that organizes nonpossessory securities is the most pronounced impediment to extending credit. There is a pressing need to introduce simpler and less expensive forms of registering mortgages and security interests. For example, the current system, which sets fees at 1.5 percent of the value for mortgaging real estate, is prohibitively expensive. Pledges on movable property are effective only if the creditors take possession of the property.

Delays in dispute resolution through the judiciary coupled by unsatisfactory compensation for losses resulting from disputes deter banks (and others) from diversifying their business portfolios and from assuming more aggressive stances in the market. The irresolute judiciary system in Egypt is repeatedly cited as the strongest constraint on business transactions. The role of banks in availing capital to private businesses could easily multiply and diversify if the capacity of the Egyptian judiciary system for resolving disputes were strengthened.

Two sets of regulations governing investment companies and joint-stock companies place limitations on their ability to diversify their investments and financial instruments. The General Authority for Investment (GAFI) does not allow investment companies to place investments with values higher than their paid-in capital. This restriction limits the leverage capacity of these firms and discourages innovation in managing investments. Secondly, existing joint-stock companies are unduly denied the issuance of preferred shares if it was not originally included in their initial articles of incorporation.

Capacity to diversify the portfolios held by institutional investors to maximize returns is essential in improving the allocative efficiency of these institutions and enabling them to participate in energizing the securities market in Egypt. The bulk of the constraints on instruments diversification falls on private insurance and pension funds. For example, PCPF portfolio investments are subject to controls and approval by EISA as follows: 1) at least 25 percent must be held in the form of state-guaranteed securities; 2) no more than 15 percent in a checking account in a bank in Egypt; and 3) no more than 65 percent in real estate in Egypt.

PCPFs must also list these investments and present certifications for them, and agree not to withdraw any money except with EISA's approval. In addition, they must send to EISA documents proving that real estate purchases were convenient and free of encumbrances. They cannot sell any property without the approval of EISA.

PAPFs must also observe the following investment diversification rules:

— at least 50 percent of their portfolio must be held as deposits in the NIB;
— 10 percent, as a maximum, in debentures with fixed interest;
— 10 percent, as a maximum, in shares of Egyptian companies;
— 10 percent, as a maximum, in demand deposits in public sector banks;

— 10 percent, as a maximum, in housing units in Egypt, to be built or owned by members of the fund;
— no limit on notes with government warranty;
— no limit on deposits in public sector banks.

PROPOSALS FOR FINANCIAL SECTOR REFORM TO FOSTER PSD

The Egyptian government's recent financial sector reforms—such as discontinuing the system of administrative allocation of bank credit, the liberalization of interest rates and foreign exchange markets, and the introduction of the new Capital Markets Law 95 of 1992—have enhanced the allocative efficiency of the financial sector and have paved the way for easier participation by private firms in that sector. Yet the task is not complete. Further deregulation measures need to be taken by reducing financial repression, relaxing barriers to entry, granting autonomy to intermediary institutions, and creating a competitive, level playing field for all players. Such measures will advance the development of an efficient, diversified, and solvent financial sector that would be able to cater to the private sector need for capital.

The reform agenda put forward by the American Chamber of Commerce in Egypt is presented below. This agenda was put together by a task force composed of members with varied banking, finance, business, and other professional backgrounds. The task force drew on the experience of the chamber's membership and the records of many exchanges and discussions held with public officials and other businessmen in Egypt and internationally.

Financial sector reforms normally come with serious budgetary and monetary implications which need to be studied carefully before one commits to a fixed agenda. This task is best handled by a private–government task force charged with financial sector reform. It is expected that substantial expert analysis will be needed to support the discussion and elaboration of the final agenda.

Foster mobilization of domestic financial resources

1. Remove or reduce financial repression resulting from low interest rates on domestic public liabilities such as social security, insurance, and pension funds held by the NIB; allow private financial intermediaries to compete for those funds.
2. Reward mandatory reserve requirements held by the CBE from the financial sector institutions with progressively improving interest rates.

3. Allow proprietorships and simple partnerships to set aside reserves that could be excluded from the taxable personal income of their owners, in the same way as corporate companies are allowed to retain earnings before distribution of profits.

Enable financial intermediary institutions

4. Eliminate the distinction between 'commercial banks' and 'investment banks' which prescribes a minimum of 51 percent Egyptian ownership in commercial banks.
5. Eliminate discrimination between bank-owned mutual funds and other private mutual funds insofar as restriction on leveraging is concerned (20:1 and 10:1, respectively).
6. Allow private nonbank mutual funds to issue multiple funds and open-ended funds to equate them with bank-owned mutual funds.
7. Remove the minimum capital requirement bias favoring fund-management companies managing mutual funds over those managing portfolios.
8. Eliminate the 1:1 limitation on the ratio of investment to capital (paid-in) set by GAFI for investment companies.
9. Revise the $15 million minimum capital required for licensing a bank to operate in Egypt so that it would not apply to branches of international banks with strong capital positions.
10. Relax the restrictions on the entry of new banks to make it subject to objective criteria such as minimum capital, financial strength of owners, and detailed business plans.
11. Relax the criteria set by EISA for the entry of new private insurance companies and private pension funds to be based only on objective prudential regulations of solvency, adequate accounting standards, and financial disclosure requirements/transparency; and remove controls on premium rates, discounts, and commissions.
12. Allow foreign insurance firms to enter the Egyptian market to compete on a level playing field with domestic ones.

Stimulate instrument diversification

13. Remove quota and compulsory allocations set by EISA on the investment portfolios of the insurance companies and pension funds.
14. Remove ex ante authorization by EISA of transactions and investments made by pension funds and replace it by effective supervisory mechanisms and reporting/disclosure requirements.
15. Allow the operation of a second tier of brokers with higher capitalization requirement (existing requirement is LE250,000)

and authorize them to extend credit to clients and hold accounts consisting of cash and securities.

16. Allow brokers that meet the second-tier capital requirements to have custody of securities in their 'street name' to facilitate settlement of trading.
17. Remove requirement of on-the-spot basis trading to allow for the introductions of futures and options.
18. Adopt the issuance of government notes and bonds (in lieu of treasury bills) to demonetize the deficit and create long-term liquidity.
19. Adjust tax liability for individuals to remove bias against debt financing (the tax law allows deductions against dividend income equal to 20 percent of face value of equity, or 10 percent if not publicly subscribed, versus none on bonds).

Reform institutions, regulations, and practices that affect transaction costs

20. Discontinue the announcement of bankers' tariff guidelines made by the CBE and impose penalties on collusive behavior.
21. Eliminate or reduce stamp duties on loans and overdrafts.
22. Reduce mortgage registration fees and make it a service fee rather than a tax.
23. Discontinue the announcement of CBE guidelines for banks' monthly commission charges.
24. Deregulate brokers' commissions (currently fixed at 1 percent, although discounts are offered on large deals) and allow competitive pricing of brokerage fees.
25. Remove the incentive for listing of closed-stock companies and make it voluntary only for firms with publicly traded securities. This is expected to reduce listing fees and would foster competitive behavior of stock exchanges to improve their services to listed firms and perhaps even invest in automated settlement systems which would in turn make securities transactions more efficient.
26. Strengthen dispute resolution mechanisms such as the judiciary and arbitration agents.
27. Reform the commercial code to facilitate securitization.

Eight

Linking Egypt with International Markets

The Federation of Egyptian Chambers of Commerce

INTRODUCTION

There is ample macroeconomic evidence that economies that are more open grow more quickly. The frontier of business opportunities is being expanded by openness, in order to enable Less-Developed Countries (LDCs) to function competitively in the international arena. By linking up with international firms, LDC firms are able to do so through a combination of lower operating costs, particularly in labor-intensive manufacturing, adoption of modern management techniques and practices, and better production processes. Egypt's Open Door policy of the 1970s featured some measures to promote linkages with the international markets (linkages are defined in terms of the flow of goods and capital, that is, import, export, and foreign investment inflow and outflow).

Linkages were seen as a means of modern technology transfer and took the form of attracting foreign investment in a variety of formats (joint ventures, subcontracting, partnership alliances, technical cooperation agreements, licensing, franchising, procurement contracts). The emphasis was on developing indigenous technological capabilities and nurturing domestic markets. The government's investment promotion strategy combined packages of tax holidays, credit subsidies, minimum local content requirements, custom exemption for industrial inputs, free zones, and investment in physical infrastructure (ports, new industrial communities, etc.). These promotional packages were granted to some selected sectors that were seen as important for the Egyptian economy within the context of a central national development plan. Egypt had embraced import substitution, infant-industry protection, and market administration as its fundamental policy themes.

In the 1970s, these policies were not unique to Egypt. Developing technological capability and fostering infant industries have been important aspects of development policies worldwide since World War II. A very common approach was to establish import protection for infant industries, supported by government assistance for credit, procurement, and technological support. Results were mixed. While some countries had success with infant-industry protection, the majority found themselves saddled with inefficient firms (public and private) supported by unearned 'rents.'

Successfully industrialized countries like Japan, Korea, and Taiwan did adopt an export push strategy with restrictions on imports to protect infant domestic producers and very selective licensing of foreign direct investment (FDI)—a strategy that worked in part because of the favorable world economic conditions of that time. More recently, newly industrializing Malaysia, Thailand, Singapore, Indonesia, and China opted for very different policies that were dictated largely by the shifts in the international rules of the game. Their strategies of choice centered around FDI-led exports with increasingly liberal trade regimes. For them, industry development motivated by profit, rather than bureaucratically administered markets, proved to be a more effective strategy.

There is one important observation that must be highlighted. The common strategy that both groups of countries continued to have despite the differences in their development policies is that the private sector was given central stage in investment and trade. Consequently, as the world economy evolved, the ability of the private sector in the host countries to absorb or generate new technology and differentiate products dictated the new order of the game.

For the last twenty years, the Egyptian economy was directed by the government. As a result, the private sector has not kept up with the developments made in international markets. Starting in the 1990s, Egypt has implemented an economic reform and structural adjustment program where privatization, financial liberalization, and private sector development are priorities. The economic reform program has been accompanied by trade liberalization, reduction of customs duties, and enhancement of exports. Concurrently, a number of institutions have been created to link Egypt to international markets. Altogether, these policies will promote Egypt's international competitiveness.

Yet, there remain many issues that inhibit growth in trade and FDI. What lessons can Egypt draw from its past record of performance and other countries' experiences? What benefits can it draw from linking with the world economy? And what needs to be done to align Egypt's economy with the new rules of the game?

These are some of the questions that this chapter explores. Special attention is given to the constraints on the private sector's capacity to participate in linking Egypt with the international markets. Current efforts to promote trade and FDI in Egypt are generally outlined and specific recommendations are offered.

GAINS FROM TRADE AND INVESTMENT LIBERALIZATION

When developing countries were following import substitution policies, FDI was seen as a way of jumping trade barriers. Under these circumstances, FDI can be welfare reducing. Today, FDI is increasingly being used to enhance export capabilities. According to recent estimates, with industrialized-country tariffs and quantitative restrictions being reduced by 20 percent to 50 percent under the Uruguay Round, developing countries should experience aggregate export gains of about $70 billion (in 1990 prices), mostly in labor-intensive manufactured articles including clothing, footwear, and furniture.

Benefits of linkages

The precise effects and benefits from trade and investment liberalization will depend on the specifics of the reforms introduced by each government and its trading partners. But overall, there are five potential gains. First, there are efficiency and welfare gains. Liberalization replaces high-cost domestic goods with lower-cost foreign goods and permits consumption to expand. Both lower prices and greater consumption contribute to welfare gains.

Second, there are firm-level economies of scale. An increase in foreign competition due to liberalization reduces the markup and, in the medium term, increases the output of efficient domestic firms, which in turn reduces average cost, just as if technical progress had increased productivity.

Third, there are induced changes in foreign investment. By improving access to foreign producers' goods (including raw materials, components, and capital goods), liberalization helps to attract investment from foreign multinationals that are pursuing global production strategies. Such investment, in turn, can increase the productivity of domestic factors of production.

Fourth, there are productivity gains from trade. In addition to the initial increase in the level of output, greater openness has been observed to lead to higher long-term growth in output. The potential explanations for this phenomenon include the availability of new and specialized inputs from world markets, the possibility of continuous innovation in products and processes to improve productivity, and greater research and development by firms when their potential market is larger.

Fifth, there is positive feedback from concerted liberalization. When several countries are liberalizing at the same time, the positive effects are reinforced. In particular, terms-of-trade effects are more favorable than under unilateral liberalization, as each country's exports expand along with its imports.

According to recent estimates, with the GDP of high-income countries (including some fast-growing, non-OECD economies) rising at 2.7 percent, world trade is expected to grow in volume at a robust 5.9 percent between 1994 and 2003, and developing-country exports will tend to rise about half of a percentage point faster. World trade growth may well exceed 6 percent per annum toward the end of the 1990s as activity in Europe and Japan recovers and new trade agreements are phased in.

Effect of GATT and Uruguay Round

Studies by the GATT Secretariat suggest that the Uruguay Round will increase merchandise trade by 12 percent by the year 2005 over the level that would have existed if trade were to grow at its historical average for 1980–91 (4.1 percent). The largest increases are likely to occur in clothing (60 percent); textiles (34 percent); agricultural, forester, and fishery products (20 percent); and processed food and beverages (19 percent). Most estimates show the Uruguay agreement contributing about a 1 percent annual gain to world income over the next ten years, ranging from $200 billion to $300 billion a year (in 1992 dollars).

TRADE REFORMS IN THE 1990s

The economic costs of protection, though well known, were dramatized as the protected economies got into fiscal and balance-of-payment difficulties in the 1980s. Today, the consensus among developing nations points toward trade liberalization. Usually, a country used to regard the easing of import restrictions as a cost, to be undertaken only if compensating benefits were to be provided by its trading partners. However, unilateral trade liberalization is now proved to be effective for the developing countries.

The results of this approach have been impressive. With trade liberalization, Indonesia and Thailand have witnessed a rapid shift to manufactured exports. China has had tremendous success in building trade, especially through its special economic zones.

In the Uruguay Round of the General Agreement on Tariffs and Trade (GATT), negotiations addressed some of the issues of multilateral and unilateral trade liberalization. The GATT was concerned with three broad areas: first, increasing market access, including more open trade in agriculture and textiles (sectors that had received exceptional treatment within the GATT), and removing or reducing voluntary export restraints and orderly marketing arrangements; second, extending the GATT to new areas—principally trade in services and trade-related investment requirements imposed by governments—and enforcing intellectual property rights; and third, strengthening the GATT rules, especially those covering antidumping, subsidies, product standards, import licensing, safeguards, and dispute settlement.

The GATT agreements still contain many escape clauses, especially for developing countries, but the obligations of developing countries are also increasing. Regardless of the GATT rules in granting exemptions for the developing world, industrial countries are not going to be lenient when it comes to enforcing antidumping rules or environmental protection standards. The standards for quality of goods and services exported to industrial countries are expected to prove more demanding for developing countries. Traders that are swifter in improving quality, observing environmental standards, and reducing costs through technological innovation and efficiency will be the trade game winners in the years to come.

CURRENT EFFORTS TO PROMOTE TRADE AND FDI IN EGYPT

The current efforts undertaken by the government of Egypt include measures to establish a strong institutional and administrative base for an outward-oriented economy. Since 1990 the government has pursued ambitious economic reform within the framework of the Economic Reform and Structural Adjustment Program (ERSAP), which aims at creating an environment that fosters private sector growth in an export-oriented economy. ERSAP's objective is to move Egypt's economy away from being highly interventionist, centrally planned, and inward oriented, to being decentralized, market based, and more outward oriented, with a private sector operating in a free, competitive, and stable environment. Investment, pricing, and output decisions would be made by the business sector on the basis of market conditions and financial profitability. With regard to the specific role of the government, the ERSAP calls for an essential transition from managing and controlling production and investment to being a catalyst for private sector activity.

Trade control measures

In trade-related matters, ERSAP envisages the elimination of trade controls and the implementation of export promotion measures. Egypt used to have a lot of restrictive practices that acted as entry barriers to exporters; these are currently being dismantled. Local content requirement schemes offer reductions in customs duties on imported inputs where the reductions are linked to the proportion of locally manufactured parts in the finished exportable products. There have also been changes in the duty drawback system, which now offers immediate reimbursement of customs duties and sales taxes levied. The temporary admission system now allows for replacing letters of guarantee for an unofficial declaration by the potential importer to reexport the product that contains imported components or raw materials within a fixed time period, or else be required to pay the original duties and any pertaining interest charges. The above efforts are all directed at avoiding any additional financial costs that are incurred by the exporter.

Yet serious problems occur in the practical implementation of these policies where the practical operations at the working level are not necessarily keeping up with statements made at the top level, and huge discrepancies still exist in some areas in implementation at the microfirm level. Procedures are still very cumbersome, demand extensive documentation, take a long processing time, and have only benefited a small number of exporters.

Export development and promotion

In Egypt there are several projects, programs, and institutions aimed at, and catering to, export development and promotion that have been set up by private sector funds, multinational organizations, or international organizations. These include: the Trade Development Center (TDC); the Egyptian Export Promotion Center (EEPC); Protrade, established by the Deutsche Gesellschaft für Technische Zusammenarbeit (GTZ) in cooperation with the German–Arab Chamber of Commerce, the General Organization for International Exhibitions and Fairs, and the EEPC; and the Export Information Center, which communicates with several international data banks to source information on export opportunities available for Egyptian products. Some ministries have specific offices providing information to Egyptian exporters and importers, for example, the Ministry of Agriculture's Agrobusiness Investment Office (AIO).

Of notable significance is the Federation of Egyptian Chambers of Commerce (FECC), which has a number of objectives including the development of business opportunities and the strengthening of trade and investment relations between Egypt and international business communities. These objectives are pursued through joint councils between the FECC and counterpart organizations in each of the different countries, which meet periodically to pursue matters of mutual interest.

Also, the Egyptian Businessmen's Association (EBA) is one of the most active Egyptian organizations in strengthening the linkages of the Egyptian economy and the international markets through its Operational Unit for Transnational Approach.

Multilateral organizations also play a significant role in promoting international linkages. The United Nations Industrial Development Organization (UNIDO) has been particularly active in setting up programs to promote international subcontracting arrangements. They have opened offices in several OECD countries with the main function of matching companies in the respective OECD countries with companies in LDCs. They also help LDC companies with skills development, contract arrangements, and other assistance that may be required. Examples of efforts supported by multilateral organizations in Egypt include: the European–Egyptian Investment Promotion Program (EEIPP), which is financed by the European Economic Community; the Investment and Partnership Promotion Project recently established with the assistance of the Canadian International Development Agency (CIDA); and the Business Cooperation Network (BRE/BC-NET) established in 1988 by the Commission of the European Communities.

The general problem with these otherwise well-meaning efforts is their relatively poor development in terms of management, infrastructure, and marketing; by and large, the Egyptian private sector is unaware of the availability of these services.

Capital market development and expansion

The capital market is regarded as the backbone of economic activity and directly affects all venues of the microeconomy. Since the implementation of the ERSAP, the government of Egypt has been committed to developing and expanding the capital market and has taken several steps toward stimulating and enhancing its activities to more comprehensively meet the needs of a changing economy. These steps can be outlined as follows:

1. Providing technical assistance to the Egyptian stock market, and allowing trade of foreign stocks in Egypt and of Egyptian stocks and bonds in the foreign markets.
2. Allowing the establishment of brokerage firms and financial consulting houses that can offer the necessary support to investors trading in stocks and bonds.
3. Allowing the private sector to set up insurance companies.
4. Permitting the establishment of new foreign exchange brokering firms.
5. Issuing the capital market law—Law 59 of 1992—as a necessary step toward stimulating activity in the capital market.
6. Removing limitation on foreign banks in Egypt when dealing with Egyptian pounds.
7. Enhancing communication with foreign capital markets.
8. Amending current regulations to stimulate the capital market, for instance by allowing 'secret accounts' in Egyptian banks.

Despite these welcome efforts, there still remain several more steps that are required to further enhance linkages with foreign international markets, particularly in the area of issuance of stocks and bonds for private Egyptian firms.

ANALYSIS OF MAJOR HINDRANCES TO TRADE AND FDI LINKAGES IN EGYPT

Compared to other countries, there are relatively few linkages between Egyptian and international markets. FDI, often a major conduit to linkage development, is lower for Egypt than for countries with comparable GDPs (see Table 8-1).

FDI now represents the main financing flow to developing economies, and the primary source of private capital for low-income countries, accounting for more than one-quarter of aggregate net

Table 8-1
FDI as a percentage of GDP in Egypt and other countries

	1980	1991	1992
Malaysia	3.8	7.3	8.7
Thailand	0.6	2.2	2.1
Mexico	1.1	1.7	1.7
Argentina	1.2	1.9	1.3
Turkey	0.03	0.8	0.8
Egypt	2.4	0.7	0.8

Source: Linkages between Egyptian and Foreign Firms, FIAS, 1994

flows and exceeding total long-term debt flows. It reaches both middle- and low- income countries, both big and small, both credit-worthy and those that are less so.

FDI also helps developing countries close the technology gap with developed countries, upgrade their managerial skills, and enlarge their export markets. In the 1980s and 1990s, FDI flows have shifted from manufacturing and extractive sectors to the services sector, particularly the new capital-intensive service industries such as telecommunications, transportation, banking, and public utilities, which are currently being privatized and opened to FDI in a number of developing countries, including Egypt.

Traditional factors that attracted FDI flows to the developing world in the 1970s and early 1980s, such as low labor cost, product life cycle, and the servicing of a protected market, although still important, have weakened considerably. In many industries, the proportion of labor cost to total manufacturing cost has declined, and new patterns of the international product life cycle have developed. In light of this new environment, FDI flows have in general been attracted to developing economies with an efficient and dynamic private sector, accompanied by responsive institutions, a highly motivated skilled labor force, and a flexible financial system.

Another indicator of Egypt's weak linkages with the international markets is its relatively low degree of trade openness, as measured by its ratio of imports and exports to GDP (see Table 8-2).

There are five main issues that explain the relative weaknesses of trade and FDI linkages between Egypt and international markets: 1) the macroeconomic environment and policies; 2) the regulatory environment; 3) the infrastructural environment; 4) the private businesses; and 5) human resources.

Table 8-2
Imports and exports as a percentage of GDP in Egypt and other countries

	Exports		Imports	
	Merchandise	Goods & services	Merchandise	Goods & services
Malaysia	68.03	77.99	63.53	78.06
Mexico	11.34	15.78	13.21	17.00
Argentina	10.01	10.36	3.02	4.63
Turkey	13.48	19.68	19.17	23.07
Egypt	10.50	20.19	30.02	32.67

Source: International Financial Statistics, IMF, 1994

The macroeconomic environment and policies

Tariffs

In 1980 the tariff structure was completely reformed to link protection to manufacturing stages of production. The intention was to have raw materials taxed at rates less than intermediate goods, which were in turn taxed at rates less than final products. The effect of this reform was to institutionalize tariff escalation, a situation that was aggravated by multiple exchange rates for customs valuation. A comprehensive reform occurred in 1986, and the ensuing structure continues to serve as a foundation for current tariff policy. More recently, tariffs were reduced by 10 percent across the board and tariff categories were consolidated. The duty range of 5 percent to 160 percent was narrowed to a maximum of 70 percent in February 1994. By 1996 the government plans to reduce the maximum tariff to 40 percent. Yet the resulting tariff regime will still be 'too close' vis-à-vis other countries that compete with Egypt for both FDI and trade flows.

Taxation and investment incentives

Despite the recent improvements and relaxation in the relevant rules and procedures, the incentive system in Egypt suffers from a number of weaknesses and some inconsistencies that need to be addressed. First, the economic justification for many of the tax incentives (limited period tax holidays) is nonexistent; international evidence shows that tax exemptions are a 'bonus' but not a determinant factor in FDI decisions. Second, the budgetary cost of the incentives appears to be high, and may create an FDI deterrent of a different kind: the possibility of fiscal deficit–driven inflation. Third, the incentive system is too complex and bureaucratic: several laws and institutions are involved; the periods for tax holidays vary considerably (and tend to prove too short for firms with projects that require long periods before turning out profits); and the availability of incentives is related to an approval process, which in the case of the General Authority for Investment still requires lengthy procedures and considerable time.

The exchange rate

The exchange rate was unified in 1991 as part of the reform program for the second standby agreement with the IMF. Since the reform program, the change in the nominal exchange rate has not exceeded 2 percent. The liberalization of the exchange rate was expected to cause a major depreciation in the Egyptian pound. However, the pound to dollar exchange rate has not reached beyond the level of LE3.40 per dollar, and has appreciated by some 40 percent in real effective terms. The resulting stability, combined with interest differentials between foreign and domestic interest rates, has stimulated large capital inflows but has also discouraged exports.

The regulatory environment

In order to foster private sector development, the Egyptian authorities recently began dismantling regulatory obstacles to business entry and operation: projects with an investment cost up to LE10 million no longer require obtaining official government approvals; approval requirements for business expansions, changes in product mix, and new products were removed; legal provisions for agricultural land rental contracts were made more flexible; licensing and approval authorities relating to investors were unified in order to avoid overlapping regulatory jurisdictions by local, governorate, and central authorities; and private sector participation in distribution of certain products (cement, pesticides, fertilizers) has been allowed. Yet several regulatory impediments still hamper the development of FDI and trade linkages.

Of particular significance is what is termed the 'Egyptian Selling Price' whereby customs officials establish a price for every product the first time it enters Egypt; this sets a minimum floor price for that particular item, referred to as the 'Egyptian Selling Price.' All subsequent imports are then valued at least as much as that first shipment. The complications of this practice are staggering. They affect suppliers who are new to the Egyptian market, or who are trying to offer products at reduced prices in order to gain market share. Importers are constantly required to justify differences in product quality or production costs.

Quality control regulations also present significant difficulties. In order to comply with inspection regulations, importers must provide samples of the shipment to be imported to the General Organization for Export and Import Control. Testing is poor, inconsistent, and excessively redundant. This increases the cost of doing business and often causes loss of profit opportunities due to delays in processing through customs. Adding to these problems is the fact that the current list of products subject to inspection is too broad and the inspection fee is considered by many importers to be excessively high.

The infrastructural environment

Business support and information services

Egypt's business support industry is young and still suffers from the weaknesses that are normally associated with operating in inward-oriented protectionist markets. Both the demand for and supply of business services such as training, market research, product design and development, quality control, and so forth, leave a lot to be desired. There are firms and establishments that offer such services in Egypt but the quality of services demanded by the market is self-defeating. The costs of information and technology services remain beyond the capacity of most small- and medium-sized Egyptian businesses. The low (but slowly rising) demand for such services is explained by the lack of competitive pressure on firms to improve quality and efficiency and by the lack of economies of scale (because of inward orientation) that would otherwise allow a firm to pay for such services. Only 30 percent of small- and medium-sized Egyptian firms have ever used the services of consultants or experts to improve the production process, test quality of inputs and outputs, or develop product design. The only expert services that are sourced are the traditional ones—accounting, legal, and auditing.

Currently there exists a wealth of information services in Egypt designed to provide business decision-support data and facilitate communication with international operators in several fields. But paradoxically, in the age of communication revolution, the information gap remains a problem in Egypt like in other developing countries. A recent ILO-sponsored study on linkages in several countries confirms that inadequate information is a major problem in linkages. Private firms, especially small- and medium-size ones, do not have the information that would help them identify or evaluate potential partners, contact them, negotiate and draw up contracts, know what the market trends are, or access the most cost-effective technology.

Infrastructure and transportation costs

Egypt has a relatively well-developed physical infrastructure including updated and expanded energy and power resources; a plentiful, stable supply of electricity; readily available water; over twelve thousand kilometers of paved roads; an extensive railway; and good harbor facilities.

Because of deregulation, land transportation in Egypt is improving but weak. Poor maintenance transport vehicles and lack of equipment are negative factors that impair the distribution sector's capacity to serve the domestic and regional markets. There are also deficiencies in the shipping industry. Port costs are high due to Egyptian public sector agencies and other government monopolies that control freight unloading and storage facilities into and out of Egypt. This monopoly has led to import and export costs that are among the highest in the world and undermines Egypt's ability to compete in global markets. Demonopolization of government port services could substantially lower the cost of doing business in Egypt.

Private businesses

Formalized linkages among private manufacturers are very limited in Egypt. According to a survey of seventy-five medium-size manufacturing firms in March 1994, only 6 percent were found to have business contracts with either larger or smaller manufacturers. However, one-third reported that they sell, on average, 15 percent of their products to other manufacturers, which implies that a larger portion of interfirm transaction is done on a case-by-case basis rather than by fixed term contracts. Like domestic ones, international linkages are also weak. Only 8 percent were found to have either joint ventures or production under license with international firms. Most linkages with international firms occur in relation to importation of production machinery which very often involves training and assistance in operation and maintenance; but such linkages last only for short periods following the sale.

In an attempt to draw on the experience of international firms (especially from industrialized countries), Egyptian firms have tried to develop some linkages with them. While those who have succeeded drew valuable benefits, the process remains limited and many have had little success in finding the right partner.

Most of the burden for linkage development falls on the private sector. Normally private businessmen are expected to seize every opportunity available to them to promote their interests, short and long term. This is often the case but not always. Sometimes the business community may have been isolated and protected for so long, as is true in Egypt, that it may not be ready to venture out of its collective shell. At other times the different thought frameworks between the government and the private sector lead to a lack of proper communication, something that is not conducive to establishing a common 'business language,' a key element in attracting FDI and promoting linkages.

The low quality of products and inconsistency of quality standards is reportedly one of the major obstacles to sourcing goods for exports in Egypt. One important explanation is that production facilities are not properly maintained and in many instances are outdated. In the above-mentioned survey, the evidence suggests that Egyptian firms require some assistance in production planning and technology upgrading. Three-quarters of the surveyed firms indicated that their technologies need updating.

Human resources

The main ingredient to the economic success of a business is the quality of the people involved. The lack of qualified, skilled, and educated personnel (in both technical and professional fields) needed to deal with externalities and scale economies is one of the major hindrances to effective linkage and to the development of private businesses in Egypt. Quality personnel is one of the most important elements in an outward-oriented strategy that needs the capacity to use both local and external resources to package the technical, marketing, and managerial knowhow for entry into world markets.

Firms in Egypt cannot easily find persons that combine good technical knowledge, computer literacy, foreign languages, and good business sense. They are forced to undertake lengthy and costly training programs and quite often their newly trained personnel are siphoned off by another company, or attracted by the rich companies of the Gulf.

More than three-quarters of the firms included in the survey mentioned earlier reported that efficiency of their labor force is the second most important obstacle (after market size/economies of scale) to reducing their cost of production. Most private operators in Egypt attribute poor quality control in production to low vocational/skill levels of labor.

RECOMMENDATIONS FOR MORE EFFECTIVE LINKAGES

Despite all the efforts undertaken by the Egyptian authorities in recent times, there still remains a need for additional reform in the key problem areas analyzed in this chapter. Some recommendations are presented below.

The macroeconomic environment and policies

Tariffs

There is an urgent need to analyze the tariff structure and its effect on foreign and domestic demand for traded goods. The analysis should aim to quantitatively assess distortions on resource allocations arising from the tariff regime and the impact of trade policy and customs reforms on the structure and level of trade by sector, product, and export market. The ultimate objective should be to motivate reductions in both the dispersion of the rates of protection and the average level of tariffs. In this way, reforms should be implemented with the objective of reducing the disparity between tariffs on raw materials and capital goods and those on final goods.

Taxation and investment incentives

A more uniform and competitive tax structure is urgently needed. It is important to ensure that incentives create no new distortions in the economy. Any restrictions on FDI regarding foreign contribution, priorities, local content, and export procedures should be relaxed as much as possible, coupled with the elimination of inefficient and lengthy bureaucratic procedures to provide an environment for linkages that is appealing to foreign investors.

The exchange rate

The exchange rate system is a crucial element in the economic activity of all countries. Determination of the exchange rate should be left to the market forces without any artificial intervention from external sources. On the other hand, we need to take into consideration whether the real exchange rate reflects the international competitiveness of Egypt's non-oil exports. The determination of the real exchange rate would also need to consider other relevant variables such as tariffs, international prices for major goods, and capital and aid flows that result in the simultaneous attainment of internal and external equilibrium both in current and future periods.

The regulatory environment

Barriers to market entry should be immediately dismantled, such as the 51 percent Egyptian ownership rule that is a condition for investment in certain sectors (including tourism and banking).

Export and import procedures should be streamlined through the establishment of a centralized processing center; redundant documentation needs to be eliminated. There should at least be uniformity applied in bureaucratic procedures, to avoid the present level of confusion. The level of quality control testing—which at present is poor, inconsistent, and excessive—needs to be reformed, and the level of the inspection fee should be reconsidered.

The infrastructural environment

Business support and information services

For industries with a strong export potential and whose competitiveness has been distorted by earlier inward-looking policies, there is a need to provide targeted support, perhaps in the form of technical assistance and working capital. For small- and medium-size exporters, there is a need to develop broader access to working capital and to ensure neutral status in the competitive financial markets.

There is also a need for new institutions that can encourage competitiveness and outward orientation by providing technical and marketing support. The roles of the institutions formed to serve this objective should highlight the importance of central coordination among the multilateral organizations, chambers of commerce, industry associations, trading companies, export manufacturers, and business associations. These bodies should collaborate to form a network that enhances the opportunities available to the business community at large and promotes the local environment on the international scene. The current efforts undertaken in Egypt, which are by their nature conflicting, disjointed, and separate, only serve to weaken their final results.

Infrastructure and transportation costs

Reforms should be undertaken to decrease the costs of doing business in Egypt by gradually demonopolizing the government port services.

In addition, the present infrastructure should be improved to comply with international standards. As a result of the externalities and scale economies in infrastructure investments and the imperfection of information in the world markets, both the physical infrastructure (ports, transport, and communication) and the institutional infrastructure that are needed in Egypt must be built through a joint effort of the public and private sectors in order to effectively move toward investment-oriented development.

Private businesses

The business mentality of the different levels of government officials, in particular upper management, has to be changed with respect to their skeptical attitude toward international linkages. The prevailing view is that competition from abroad, which linkages and a more open economy imply, is dangerous and unfair in the sense that predatory practices of large profit-motivated multinationals will gobble up the smaller Egyptian firms. It is therefore essential that the traditional mentality regarding international linkages shift toward greater receptivity.

Similarly, private business leaders need to look outward rather than inward, and to consider themselves participants in the international economy rather than the Egyptian economy. This leads to the necessity of increasing mutual trust and understanding between the government and the private sector so that, through continuous dialogue, they can work together to penetrate international markets. In drawing up foreign policy, the government should place business interests among the priority issues, and should work toward removing the currently present artificial barrier between politics and economics. Current efforts in the right direction do exist, but they need to be greatly strengthened. The ultimate objective is to develop purposeful mechanisms for ongoing dialogue between the government and private businesses and to formulate a strategy for Egypt's role in the world economy.

Nine

The Industrialization of Egypt

The Federation of Egyptian Industries

INTRODUCTION AND BACKGROUND

The Egyptian government has undertaken a series of remarkable policy and regulatory reforms that have greatly enhanced Egypt's business climate, and in a way that has been particularly beneficial to the industrial sector. The government's policy changes have been effective, timely, and prudent. The changes are already making an impact as reflected in statistics that indicate a steady rise in private sector shares of employment and value of output that originates in Egyptian manufacturing. The government's leadership appears to have put into place market mechanisms that will stimulate domestic competition and link the Egyptian economy with global markets. Egypt's goal is a modern mixed economy. The government's policies are expected over time to raise the long-term productivity and the standard of living for all Egyptians. This paper supports the government's approach and addresses particular areas of its reform program which have particular importance to industrialization.

The centerpiece of the reform effort has been the government's Economic Reform and Structural Adjustment Program (ERSAP), which was launched in May 1990 to liberalize the Egyptian economy after more than thirty years of state-led centralized decision-making. The government's main reforms have been fundamental: macroeconomic stabilization, reduction of inflation, virtual elimination of the budget deficit, foreign trade liberalization, deregulation of price controls and other administrative restrictions, reorganization of public enterprises, privatization, and creation of a Social Fund for Development to alleviate the burden of adjustment on the population. The government now appears ready for entering the next stage of its policy reforms aimed at strengthening the markets, domestic competition, and international linkages.

The Egyptian industrialization problem is closely linked to the relatively small contribution of the manufacturing sector to the country's overall economic growth compared with other developing countries. Reversing the deteriorating trends for Egyptian industry requires major improvements in many areas that have been discussed earlier in this book. They include continuing macroeconomic stability; implementing antidumping measures designed to counter unfair trade practices of other countries; supporting industries over the ten-year implementation period of the General Agreement on Tariffs and Trade (GATT) 1994; demonopolizing Egyptian banking and insurance institutions; strengthening the new Capital Market Authority and encouraging the use of standardized accounting principles; privatizing the government's industrial parastatals; improving the legal and judicial framework applicable to manufacturers; adapting a low stable rate of industrial taxation; providing better business information; strengthening intellectual property rights to encourage new investments of 'higher tech' industries; increasing technology transfers; achieving higher rates of basic literacy and an improvement in the overall quality of skilled human resources; improving exports; and developing stronger, more independent trade and business associations.

The main reason for poor industrial performance lies with the preponderance of inefficient parastatals in Egyptian industry, and the inability to attract new private sector investments—particularly by medium-scale Egyptian firms and new foreign investors. As seen in the earlier chapters, a broad range of effective barriers to investment remain as a legacy of socialism, and their removal and prioritization must be addressed as part of the industrial action agenda for Egypt. The problems will not go away quickly, as evidenced by the slow progress to date on industrial privatization and the inability to curtail the continued growth of new public sector investments.

This paper highlights areas that are expected to be particularly damaging to Egyptian industrialization. The paper examines first the improved business opportunities for Egyptian industrialization locally, regionally, and internationally; second, the continued domination of manufacturing by parastatals; third, the key issues for future Egyptian industrialization under the newly completed Uruguay Round of the GATT; fourth, barriers to market development; fifth, barriers to the private sector entry into local markets; sixth, the poor services provided by infrastructure—with special attention to the Port of Alexandria; and seventh, regulatory and administrative constraints. The paper ends with a discussion of a private-sector-led industrialization strategy for Egypt, and the action agenda needed to achieve dynamic, self-sustained industrial development in the country.

Egypt's industrial environment—the geographic context and industrial structure

The local environment

Privatization efforts in industry have been slow due to fundamental difficulties. Despite increased peripheral private sector investment and substantial progress in agriculture, Egypt's economy, including manufacturing and finance, remains dominated by public sector enterprises that are effectively monopolistic. Market niches where the private sector has emerged, such as domestic wholesaling, have been dominated often by a few private firms that are effectively monopolistic and often closely aligned to public-sector vested interests. This type of market structure fails to support the competition needed to spur innovation and increase productivity. A significant improvement in the privatization effort could come about by limiting sales transactions to the stock market, rather than permitting direct purchases of public sector enterprises. Moreover, the privatization program could provide for financial support and other mechanisms to help ensure a successful drive toward private sector expansion.

The ERSAP reforms have been fundamental: exchange rates were liberalized; interest ceilings were removed; treasury bills were introduced to provide a new source of deficit finance; new import-export legislation was passed; clearance was given to governorates to sell off their small businesses which numbered more than 1,700; public assets in a few joint ventures were auctioned off and their shares floated on the Egyptian stock market; and a capital markets law was enacted to improve the ability of industrial firms to offer realistic rates on bonds. In contrast to a few years ago, currency exchange is now very easy in Egypt.

The implementation of Investment Law 230 introduced pro-industrialization features such as unrestricted ownership of investment capital; right of acquisition of land and real estate; guarantees against nationalization or confiscation of investment projects; guarantees against seizure, requisition, blocking, confiscation, custody, or sequestration of project assets and funds; safeguards against expropriation of real estate or property; and legal guarantees to open foreign currency accounts, to repatriate profits, to reexport invested capital, and to dispose of invested funds.

Egypt now has five public free zones in Nasr City, Alexandria, Port Said, Suez, and Ismailia, and some more have been announced and are under development. Individual companies can also organize themselves as free zones. Free zones have the following incentives: 100 percent corporate income tax exemption in perpetuity; 100 percent exemption on personal income tax of expatriates; 100 percent tax exemption on declared dividends; unrestricted repatriation of capital and earnings; duty free import of raw materials, production inputs, and consumer goods; duty and tax free export of free zone products to third countries; unrestricted sales to local markets subject to payment of normal applicable import duties; 50 percent reduction in applicable import duties if Egyptian components, including labor, constitute 40 percent or more of the manufactured product; freely negotiated terms of employment between worker and employer, subject to the minimum wage requirement; exemption from national social security laws if private social security benefits offered are deemed better; exemption from mandatory labor representation requirements and other provisions; unrestricted access to and control over foreign exchange holdings; qualification of firms for Export Processing Zones (EPZ) status regardless of location; and security of invested capital (Egypt has guarantees in its laws, including, the provisions of bilateral investment treaties with the United States, Great Britain, France, and other countries).

The regional environment

The Suez Canal and Egypt's favorable location adjacent to Arab and African countries provide it substantial regional trade and investment opportunities. These nearby countries, like Egypt, are opening up their economies to trade and investments by moving away from the inward-oriented socialism of the past. Egypt's position within the oil-rich Arab world offers substantial financial potential as these countries seek to diversify their investment portfolios beyond the frontiers of their own economies. Foreign investors and traders have created a highly competitive regional environment which offers a challenge to Egyptians wishing to compete in Egypt or in its regional markets. Failure to deal with problems curtailing Egyptian productivity and competitiveness will certainly lead to losses in market share for most Egyptian products.

Most importantly, the new Middle East peace initiatives appear to be offering unprecedented new opportunities for investment in Egypt.

The region is safer and thus more attractive to risk-averse investors. Also, new trade and investment opportunities are opening up with Jordan and Palestine. Chances of future trade with Lebanon and Syria are much improved. Egypt appears now to be in a position to take advantage of these new opportunities by developing industries that are competitive with those of its neighbors once the appropriate business environment becomes established.

The international environment

There appears to be substantial opportunities opening up for Egyptian industry that stem from the recently completed Uruguay Round of the GATT negotiations. Despite these apparent improvements in the international 'rules of the game,' the prevalent feeling in Egypt is mixed. Developed countries dominate international trade and keep developing countries from markets and raw materials through their systems of quotas and trade restraints. For example, Egyptian food processors and exporters often ship produce to the U.S., Australia, and Japan, because of European restrictions on processed food imports. The current international situation facing Egypt has been further exacerbated by the world recession of the last few years that has led to a slowdown in the rate of import expansion by the industrialized countries, and a concurrent deceleration in the growth rate of their demand for exports from developing economies. This slowdown has stymied Egyptian exports and has contributed to Egypt's high rate of unemployment. This situation has deteriorated as developed countries further protected their own markets in the light of their own poor performance. For Egyptians, it seems unjust and inequitable that the trade barriers of developed countries appear to be rising while those same countries are advocating the removal of trade barriers in the developing world.

The industrial structure

Despite the improving business climate and investment opportunities, Egyptian manufacturing continues to experience substantial obstacles curtailing private sector investment and growth. Even though the private sector's share of value of production and employment in manufacturing is increasing, parastatals still dominate most Egyptian industrialization. In manufacturing, Egyptian parastatals accounted for over two-thirds of the value of production and three-fourths of employment in larger scale firms and the department-store

Table 9-1
Public sector holding companies in Egypt, 1993

Holding company	Number of affiliated companies
Spinning, weaving, and ready-made clothing	17
Consumer goods	17
International trade and cotton	22
Engineering industries	22
Metallurgical industries	17
Mining, refractories, and building materials	19
Chemical industries	24
Food industry and distribution	24
Rice and flour mills	20
Agricultural development and animal wealth	20
Public works and land reclamation	13
Construction and urbanization	26
Construction and electricity distribution	16
Housing, tourism, and cinema	21
Nile and inland transportation	12
Maritime transportation	13
Pharmaceutical and medical appliances	11
Total	314

component of retail trade in 1989/90. The range of public sector industrial activities is broad, as indicated in Table 9-1 by the names of the seventeen holding companies and their 314 affiliated companies as of 1993.

Over the past decade, however, the private sector performed better than the public sector in terms of labor productivity. Employment in the private manufacturing sector grew at an average rate of about 3.8 percent per annum between 1981/82 and 1988/89, compared with the corresponding growth rate in the public manufacturing sector of 2.3 percent per annum. In 1988/89, labor productivity in the private sector was about 33 percent higher than in the public sector. In the past decade, production in the private manufacturing sector grew at about 11 percent per annum in real terms, compared with about 3 percent per annum in the public sector.[1]

Despite the overwhelming control of Egyptian manufacturing by the public sector, the private sector has been successful in some areas, and, in a few manufacturing sectors, parastatals have been pushed into a minority position by the more efficient and dynamic private sector and joint venture firms. For example, the parastatal producing air-conditioners and home appliances is now effectively bankrupt and has been displaced in the market by several private and joint venture producers. Manufacturing of plastic articles is now largely a private sector activity, producing 87 percent of the value of production in 1988/89, with individual firms established and dominating in particular niches. In automobile assembly capacity, the public sector is now in the minority.

Yet as a result of the public sector's domination of Egyptian manufacturing under socialism, the industrial structure is still characterized by a remarkable lack of smaller medium-sized firms.

Toward a new competitive model for industrialization

The Egyptian market structure is not competitive, suggesting substantial inefficiency and low productivity. The largest share of Egypt's domestic investment in technology R&D is undertaken by the public sector. This contrasts sharply with the Asian Tigers and other successfully developing countries which have enjoyed generally rising industrial productivity, most of which can be attributed to new, more productive, private sector industrial technologies.

The concept of liberalized prices among domestic rivals is distorted in Egypt's industrial sector. A free price does not mean that it is determined by markets; rather it means that the price in question is not being set by a ministerial decree. The prices of goods produced by Egyptian companies are 'free' in the sense that prices are now set by the individual producing companies rather than by a supervisory ministry. In reality, the pricing policy of public sector companies is usually subject to close scrutiny by their respective government holding companies. In addition, all enterprises are subject to a variety of regulations that affect pricings, and these multiple regulations remain operational today.

The need for new directions in policy reform can been seen by examining the government's efforts to achieve price liberalization. Price liberalization was initially advocated as a policy tool for introducing economic rationality into the allocation of resources, particularly in agriculture. In the cotton sector, price liberalization meant raising prices, but now it implies freedom for textile producers to move prices up and down in response to changes in the world market. For public sector industrial producers, price liberalization also meant price increases in order to reduce the drain of their financial deficits on the public budget. Now they are free to set their own prices in a highly cartelized domestic market, within the limits permitted by the prices of imports after customs duties. Prices are still set by agreement among producers, the holding companies to which they are attached, the Public Enterprise Office, and the Ministry of the Business Sector. As price subsidies disappear, the focus should be shifting from price liberalization to market liberalization.

Raising industrial productivity

On the basis of the experiences of other successfully developing countries, the central goal of the government's industrialization policy should be to encourage the development of cost-effective resource utilization, including land, labor, capital, infrastructure, technology, and entrepreneurship, which will lead toward high and rising levels of productivity and efficiency. The experience of the Asian Tigers and other successfully developing countries shows that export-led industrial development is critical to supporting economic expansion and higher standards of living. In all successfully developing countries over the past two decades, economic takeoff has been associated with export-led industrial growth.

To take advantage of these new opportunities, the Federation of Egyptian Industries (FEI) has identified key constraints to industrialization. Generally, FEI policies support removal of government intervention because it is not necessary, not effective, and not cost effective. Government intervention (particularly in direct production), while inherent under socialism, is less appropriate under a market economy. The potential for a private-sector-led industrial expansion in Egypt has been underscored in a recent study by the FEI. It found that an improved business environment that may stimulate new investment of about LE10 billion a year in the industrial sector and full utilization of the public sector upon being fully privatized could initially generate a 5 percent a year output expansion in general; in the medium term, that output growth could reach 8 percent a year.

The FEI is committed to improving industrial productivity and competitiveness by strengthening the government-controlled 'rules of the game,' by increasing domestic competition in an appropriate business environment, and by linking domestic commodities and investments to global markets. The ultimate aim is to improve the Egyptian standard of living. To achieve industrial growth, Egypt must be continually upgrading. This requires access to outside technologies and involves a process of constant adaption, development, improvement, and innovation within existing industries. Egypt must begin continuously upgrading its capacity to compete successfully in new industries. New business formation is needed to create jobs for new persons entering the work force, to replace jobs freed up by productivity gains in other successful industries, and to replace jobs lost in less productive industries.

The government's policy toward manufacturing should be to stimulate industrial dynamism, and this task involves lowering the cost of doing business abroad. It also involves determining economic niches in which Egypt has a global or regional comparative advantage. Defining national economic goals in terms other than long-term productivity growth is a fundamental error that would lead to inappropriate policies. Efforts to preserve all industries, as was done in the past under socialism, will stunt efforts to raise the Egyptian standard of living.

The central economic concern of Egyptian industrialization should be the capacity of the Egyptian economy to upgrade, to take advantage of its international comparative advantage, and to raise its productivity and create new and higher paying jobs. This approach necessitates that Egyptian industry become more private-sector oriented, more outward oriented, and more globally competitive in an appropriate business environment. There are three factors against which the Egyptian industrial sector needs to be safeguarded. First is excessive public sector charges. Currently high charges inhibit efficient resource allocation and contribute to high production costs and low productivity of many industries in Egypt. Second is unfair trading practices by foreign competitors. To protect domestic industries, antidumping measures need to be adopted, and appropriate action must be taken within the rules of the GATT to counter the effects on industries being hurt by foreign dumping actions. Finally, there is the continued growth of public sector investments in the industrial sectors and the monopoly position of parastatals in numerous industries. Firm entry into industrial niches dominated by the public sector is limited since private sector firms are unwilling to compete with public sector counterparts. Major segments of industrial activity are thus subject to monopoly or oligopoly behavior, which inhibits efficient resource allocation and contributes to high production costs and low productivity. At the same time, there is substantial evidence of expanding parastatal activity, which may offset the recent gains in privatization. Effective privatization cannot take place while new parastatals enter the markets or existing ones expand their investments in industrial sectors.

To counter the loss of industrial competitiveness resulting from these three factors, and to develop proactive industrialization measures in Egypt, the government should support industrial development in targeted geographic zones and industries. Support can take many forms, directly through industry subsidies and reduced financial charges, or indirectly through improved training facilities, support of research and development, improvement of information facilities, and minimal public service charges. These measures are particularly important in the short and medium term, while industries are adjusting to the rapidly changing circumstances in the local, regional, and global markets.

Experience has shown that small- and medium-sized enterprises, including those in joint ventures and subcontracting arrangements with foreign investors, are often the major source of increased exports and employment in successfully developing countries which have undertaken an export-oriented, market-driven development strategy. Egypt's problems are related to its transition toward market forces, privatization, and export-led development. These require a solution to the negative aspects of public sector dominance and national protection of manufacturing. There is a need to follow through with current industrial strategy and to continue redesigning new industrial policies, using integrated planning based on scientific technologies. The FEI, as representative of public and private Egyptian industrialization, should play a crucial role in developing the overall strategy and its implementation.

BARRIERS TO MARKET CREATION AND FIRM ENTRY AND EXIT

Different market models predict different degrees of economic efficiency, suggesting a causal relationship between market structure and market performance. One of the key indicators of a noncompetitive market structure is the scope and effectiveness of barriers to entry. This section examines some barriers that have an impact on Egyptian industrialization. These anticompetitive barriers are further reinforced by the regulatory and administrative barriers discussed later. The section begins by examining two fundamental flaws in Egypt's legal and judicial underpinnings that have undermined the general efficiency of the market for Egyptian industrialization and for the economy as a whole.

Legal and judicial obstacles

If Egypt is to be successful in creating a modern economy, the market mechanism must make economic decisions automatically. The role of the public sector will be necessarily reduced, establishing an environment that facilitates market transactions. The public sector's primary role will instead be to determine the 'rules of the game' for the economy and provide for their modification, arbitration, and enforcement. This responsibility mandates three fundamental roles for the public sector: preserving law and order, which the public sector does; enforcing contracts, which is not yet fully operational; and defining and protecting property rights, which is not yet fully implemented.

These three fundamental tasks are necessary for the government to stimulate its private sector market economy. A modern, productive market economy cannot be created if the public sector fails in any one of the above three roles. Since the second and third of these three roles are not yet in force, it is not so surprising that efforts to activate private-sector manufacturing in Egypt have failed, despite remarkable economic stabilization, up-front financial liberalization, and other reforms mentioned earlier. Failure to enforce contracts and define property rights represents possibly the most fundamental flaw in the Egyptian development effort to date.

Limiting public sector action to just these three roles could be described as a laissez-faire economic policy. It minimizes the role of the public sector while maximizing the role of the individuals. However, a laissez-faire economy would not maximize Egyptian social welfare. The Egyptian economy has many situations characterized as market imperfections, such as monopoly power in certain industrial sectors, inadequate information dissemination, and inadequate public service facilities. Without these, markets fail to bring about an optimal allocation of society's resources. For example, reliance on markets leads to too much pollution and too little R&D, physical infrastructure, and specialized industrial factors. When the self-interest of individual Egyptians differs from the interests of society, government intervention becomes necessary.

Enforcement of contracts

With regard to enforcement of contracts, the Commercial Code of 1883 and Civil Code of 1948 are the fundamental laws governing commercial transactions and contracts in Egypt. They are outdated and do not provide a sufficient legal framework for many modern forms of credit transactions and contracts. Accordingly, a comprehensive review and modernization of civil and commercial codes should be carried out in comparison with the best current international business and financial practices.

Defining property rights

With regard to defining property rights, there is a need to provide for modern, inexpensive forms of registering mortgages and security interests. In most states of the United States, the Uniform Commercial Code, as well as the modern commercial laws of many other countries, allows for a system whereby a security interest or mortgage can be perfected with respect to any form of property—whether real or personal, movable or immovable, tangible or intangible—simply by registration of the mortgage or security agreement in the public register maintained by the state. Priority of creditors registering security interests with respect to the same assets is determined by date of registration. Flexibility flows from allowing mortgages or security interests in any form of property to be registered by a creditor or entity. It is not restricted to banks, unlike the situation in Egypt with respect to commercial mortgages under Law 11 of 1940. Registration protects the public by enabling any subsequent creditor to know which property has already been mortgaged by the proposed debtor–mortgagor.

Under Egypt's commercial and civil codes and related laws, mortgages are highly restricted with respect to the property that can be mortgaged, the method of perfecting the mortgage, and who can be the beneficiary of the mortgage. Thus real estate mortgages are provided for under Egyptian law but, at the same time, are prohibitively expensive to register. With respect to a particular piece of movable or personal property, nonpossessory security interests are possible only in highly restricted circumstances, unlike the U.S. Uniform Commercial Code, where they are generally available to all bank and nonbank creditors and are easily perfected.

The real estate mortgage registration fees are prohibitively expensive. Under the civil code, mortgages of immovable property such as real estate are provided for, and can be registered with, the land register, as in many other countries. It can be registered by any bank or nonbank creditor and, in this respect, follows the usual rates and procedures of mortgages everywhere with respect to registration and foreclosure. The problem with mortgages on real estate in Egypt is the heavy cost for registering, a mortgage. Mortgage registration fees are equivalent to 1.5 percent of the amount which is being secured by the mortgage. Accordingly, a mortgage to secure a debt of LE10 million will cost LE150,000 to register.

Because of this high cost for land mortgage registration, creditors attempt to avoid paying this amount by undertaking all steps necessary except registration. Alternatively, they may seek to secure the loan by other means such as pledges of valuable personal property or by bank guarantees. This substantially raises transaction costs for credit and thereby reduces access to credit for smaller newer enterprises in favor of larger, better-established firms. Accordingly, the high percentage fees now required for mortgage registration should be replaced by reasonable flat fees.

The state of the judicial system

Egypt's legal system itself, which is the heritage of the pre-1952 monarchical regime as modified by more than thirty years of Egyptian socialism, places many constraints on the development of a market economy, thus indirectly affecting production and supply availability. Despite measures since 1991 to liberalize domestic prices and foreign trade, reform public sector enterprises, and improve the legal, judicial, and regulatory framework, many obstacles continue to hinder the operation of markets and private sector economic activity. These problems are further exacerbated by a wide range of legal and judicial constraints imposed by the commercial legal system; these contraints fall under the following categories:

1. Case delays, judgment enforcement difficulties, inadequate arbitration rules;
2. Inadequate university legal education system;
3. Lack of post-degree continuing education for judges, lawyers, and officials;
4. Inadequate legal information systems;
5. Antiquated commercial law institutions, e.g. the Commercial Register;
6. Outmoded laws, e.g. the Civil and Commercial Codes;
7. Lack of institutionalized economic law and policy analysis;
8. Lack of institutionalized private sector input on economic legislation;
9. Inadequate post-enactment public education on commercial laws;
10. Need of post-enactment monitoring of commercial laws;
11. Incomplete law reforms.

Each of these categories contains a myriad of specific constraints. For example, a fuller delineation of the first category (case delays) includes: a severe shortage of judges and lawyers experienced, specialized, and trained in commercial law matters resulting from the thirty-year socialist period; powerful incentives to delay cases because of inadequate compensation for inflation, actual attorneys fees or litigation costs, and lack of effective sanctions for frivolous delays; lack of modern effective case administration and scheduling methods; overreliance by courts on government appointed experts; and easy opportunities and incentives to appeal.

Public sector monopolies

Since the 1980s, the government has begun to ease the barriers to the private sector's entry into industries that were earlier reserved for the public sector. Yet the Egyptian economy, particularly the manufacturing sector, is still largely controlled by the relatively small number of public sector–owned enterprises which do not actively compete with each other in product markets.

Regulation of industrial competition through such policies as maintaining an effective state monopoly, controlling firm entry, or fixing prices usually works against the upgrading of competitive advantage. It also stifles competition and innovation. Under such conditions, firms become preoccupied with dealing with regulations and protecting what they have. Regulation of competition frequently makes the industry lose dynamism and innovation, as reflected in less advanced and less sophisticated need for inputs, and results in the provision of less innovative new products or services to domestic consumer industries. Deregulation of competition and privatization of state monopolies, in contrast, usually encourage national industries, stimulating competition and providing new opportunities for industrial linkages. For example, telecommunication services became very innovative in the United States after the breakup of AT&T. Yet deregulation and privatization will not succeed without active domestic rivalry. A strong antitrust policy is necessary to insure the desired effect, particularly as privatization takes place or new private sector firms economically overpower old parastatals.

There is therefore a need for action to counter public sector monopolies in the following areas: acceleration of privatization, control of expansion of investments by government-owned enterprises, removal of barriers to entry and exit, and decontrol of the remaining sectors of the economy dominated by the public sector.

As mentioned earlier, there is substantial evidence of expanding parastatal activity, which may offset the recent gains in privatization. The ultimate aim of privatization is to direct an increasing proportion of resources to the private sector. It is thus incomplete to include conditions on privatization (in a sector such as finance or textiles), or to leave open the possibility that Egypt might create new parastatals or substantially expand existing parastatals in other areas.

Private sector monopolies

The private sector is quickly becoming large enough to create serious problems of monopoly or oligopoly, particularly in the important distribution markets. The legal framework for dealing with these monopoly issues, and the related issues of unfair competition, consumer protection, and trade liberalization, is weak. There are gaps in Egypt's legislative framework for protecting market mechanisms and free competition. For example, although Law 241 of 1959 prohibits monopolies in connection with the distribution of locally made products, there is no comprehensive law against monopolies and monopolistic practices or restrictive trade practices. Egypt badly needs an anti-trust law, supported by effective and efficient institutions for its enforcement.

PHYSICAL INFRASTRUCTURE[2]

Egypt has a relatively well-developed infrastructure to support its industrial development efforts. There are, however, problems with the services provided, as illustrated below for the Port of Alexandria.

Importance of infrastructure

The type, quality, and user cost of the infrastructure currently available in Egypt negatively affects the country's international competitiveness. This includes the transportation system, the communication system, mail and parcel delivery, payments or funds transfer, and so on. Expanding and developing infrastructure is a critical part of developing productivity. There is a need to entice investment, build and expand infrastructure, establish new industrial cities, and expand small- and medium-scale industries to raise production capacity and lower unemployment.

While the physical infrastructure itself is satisfactory in Egypt, the quality of its service at many facilities is extremely poor. The facilities are run as public sector bureaucracies without private sector competition, and this leads to substantial informal costs. The Egyptian public sector has separate monopolies for shipping, stevedoring, warehousing, and other port services, as well as for airport services.

These inadequate service facilities are particularly damaging to Egyptian industrial efficiency and productivity. Despite a favorable geographical location for international trade, Egypt's transport costs to European markets exceed those of Cyprus, Greece, Israel, Turkey, and other nearby competitor countries. The root cause lies with an institutional or 'market' structure that is dominated by state-run monopolies.

The Port of Alexandria: A case in point

Probably the most damaging physical infrastructure impediment to Egyptian industry is the extremely inefficient Port of Alexandria. The high transit trade costs through the Port of Alexandria undermine Egypt's ability to compete in global markets, and they add to the costs of imports. The high costs of trade tends to lower Egyptian productivity, exports, technology transfers, employment, and foreign exchange earnings. The continuing presence of this inefficient parastatal undermines public sector credibility with private sector manufacturers and exporters. Other countries which had similar government transit trade monopolies have generally switched to more competitive private sector modes of operations for the provision of services, and this in turn has led to lower cost and more efficient services.

Egypt's current shipping system is a complex monopoly, and appears closely tied to a half dozen owners of ships carrying the Egyptian flag. Buying or selling a ship with an Egyptian flag requires the approval of the Minister of Transportation. The advantage of having a ship with an Egyptian flag is that, by law, it is possible to be one's own shipping agent and thus avoid the costly procedures associated with the monopolized public sector shipping agency. Egyptians owning ships with an Egyptian flag are in effect part of the 'monopoly' that also comprises the public sector shipping agency. According to Alexandrian importers and exporters, the fees charged by the shipping agency are mostly for services not rendered. There are approximately twenty administrative steps, mostly costs that are not technically justified.

REGULATORY AND BUREAUCRATIC ENVIRONMENT

The process of complying with formalities and regulations, or bureaucratic red tape, is considered to be an integral part of conducting business in Egypt. As such, it has a major impact on private sector development in terms of time, cost, and productivity. Indeed, numerous licenses and registrations are required at both the district and national level to start up and maintain daily business operations, and businesses must also follow certain procedures to undergo organizational changes and closures. Since 1991, the extent of direct intervention in the economy by the public sector through laws and decrees has been reduced, but considerable work remains for the market system to operate effectively.

Domestic regulatory and bureaucratic procedures permeate all areas of business in Egypt. The most commonly cited problem areas are the excessively regulatory labor law and the highly restrictive legal framework for securitization. Other problematic areas are the legal system's strong bias toward procedural rather than punitive means of compliance; the excessively restrictive system for market entry, operations, and exit regulations; and the inadequacies inherent in public institutions resulting from overburdened and underpaid staff working in overcrowded and poorly maintained facilities having inappropriate information and data-processing systems.

Several of these areas have already been discussed elsewhere. The issues regarding market entry, operations, and exit have been treated in the previous section, and legal impediments are treated elsewhere in this book. Nevertheless, it is important to underscore those problems that particularly affect the industrialization process and whose remedy would help to lay the foundation for private-sector-led industrialization in Egypt.

Public sector intervention to foster employment and regulate labor relations has become a major deterrent to doing business in Egypt, and it has acted as a disincentive to the development of labor-intensive industries where the country has a comparative advantage. Current regulations set out specific steps that must be followed in the hiring process. Termination of employment for disciplinary reasons, for example, is extremely difficult, making dismissals virtually impossible. Consequently, employers often resort to informal termination payment arrangements. Only in the case of company closures due to force majeure are employee dismissals possible, but the process must be approved by an interministerial 'stoppage committee.' Similar regulatory procedures dominate company labor relations and industrial safety committees. The provisions of the law are so detailed that compliance with each of the provisions is a highly time-consuming process that discourages labor-intensive industries from operating in the country.

As mentioned earlier, entry regulations remain highly restrictive throughout Egypt. The three-stage process required for a business to become operational constitutes a costly barrier to private sector efficiency. The first stage involves investment activity licensing (for companies with more than LE10 million in capital). A series of steps then lead up to the second stage of the process, legal incorporation. The third stage involves the establishment of the company and the purchase of operating licenses. Not only are specific actions required by all prospective owners at both the national and local level to enable a business to operate legally, but the procedures that business owners must follow are usually dictated by the type of activity of the particular business. Once processing of numerous licenses and registrations at both the local and national level are completed, there is an eventual culmination in the approval of an operating license. The ability to enter the market is crucial to private sector development because companies must continually overcome many obstacles as the procedure of registration advances. Likewise, recurrent obligations involve a cumbersome process of renewing licenses and registrations.

Closing a business that is not in bankruptcy also involves a series of steps to liquidate assets and liabilities. Unfortunately, all the pitfalls that typically present themselves are, in fact, characteristic of the Egyptian commercial system, and they represent obstacles to private sector growth. Closing a business by choice is a different matter from that related to bankruptcy, and while not nearly as complicated, it nonetheless involves extensive paperwork. Common causes for voluntary exit from the market include: expiration of the time frame for business operations that the company established in its bylaws; achievement of the company's objective; and the impossibility of company compliance with public sector rules and regulations. Fortunately, most private sector business persons in Egypt have learned to cope with the problems encountered by such difficulties and eventually, albeit inefficiently, accomplish the ultimate goal of formally constituting a business, maintaining operations, and closing activities.

In addition to complying with the numerous and recurrent regulations as part of the initiation and operation of a business, exporters and importers must obtain additional certifications and licenses that are part of the trade process. The administrative process of complying with customs regulations and the resulting bureaucratic red tape is considered by many Egyptian export and import businesses to be an important impediment to international trade in terms of time, cost, and productivity. While important reforms have been implemented since 1986 that reflect the public sector's move to a more open trade policy, numerous problems remain that give rise to a lack of transparency in trade-related activities. These problems are also apparent in the area of foreign direct investment, where despite large promotional efforts made by the government, bureaucracy remains a key obstacle to growth.

The government has also recognized that problems exist for exporters and importers and, as part of the ERSAP, it has initiated reforms aimed at improving the efficiency of customs procedures and reducing public sector revenue losses. The general objectives of the trade policy and customs reform programs include the simplification and harmonization of regulations, the improvement of the efficiency of administrative procedures, the reduction of fraudulent practices and contraband, and the overall improvement of bureaucratic regulations.[3]

GATT 1994: INDUSTRIALIZATION OPPORTUNITIES OR LOSSES?

The experience of East Asian countries and other successful developing countries shows that export-led industrial development is critical to achieving a sustainable economic expansion in countries like Egypt. The growing openness of the Egyptian economy has paralleled that which has taken place in the world economy, and the successive reductions of trade barriers resulting from the GATT agreements may contribute to that process by allowing countries to take advantage of the scale economies that result from broader markets and the globalization of production in the industrialization process. Yet the effects of these agreements on Egypt are questioned by businessmen in the country because it remains unclear what the specific industry opportunities will be.

The recent GATT agreement resulting from the Uruguay Round continues earlier efforts to liberalize trade by reducing tariffs, and it expands its coverage to include services, textiles and clothing, international investment, subsidies and countervailing measures, antidumping safeguards, and intellectual property rights. This last 'megaround' therefore widens the scope of liberalization well beyond past efforts, and sets the foundations for a broad-based expansion of activities in the global economy and in Egypt's overall trade and development strategy.

For Egypt's industrialization process, the 1994 GATT agreements could support efforts to develop those areas in which the country has a comparative advantage, it could encourage foreign investment and technological diffusion, and it could allow industries to develop economies of scale by increasing their access to larger global markets. Of particular importance to Egypt in the industrial sector are textiles and clothing, chemicals, home appliances, agro-industries, leather goods, and electronics. In the short run, the increased market access could generate a greater demand for existing industrial capacity; in the medium term, it could stimulate an expansion in investment and technological improvements that would lead to cost-effective procedures, economies of scale, and increased competitiveness in existing industries; and, in the long run, it could permit the greater international mobility of goods and services and encourage the development of new industries.

The effects of the GATT could also be disruptive to the industrialization process of the country. Under the present environment, Egyptian industries confront high production costs that make them less competitive than those in other countries. The liberalization of commerce without the reduction or elimination of the causes of those high costs could lead to a deterioration of the domestic industrial structure in this country. The result could be unintended and unanticipated structural adjustments that create a large number of unemployed workers.

Under the 1994 GATT agreements, Egypt qualifies for special and differential treatment as a developing country, but it does not qualify as a least-developed country, for which many of the terms of the agreements are not binding. Egypt is therefore in a position to possibly benefit from the liberalization of the global economy, but it must itself become part of that liberalization process. Already there have been important advances in this process. At the beginning of 1994, the maximum tariff was lowered from 80 percent to 70 percent, and maximum tariff rates are to decrease gradually by 10 percentage points until the maximum rate declines to 50 percent.

Increased market access for industrial products under the 1994 GATT agreements will result from broad-based reductions in tariffs and the removal of quantitative restrictions. For Egypt, those reductions in import barriers by its trading partners could provide an opportunity for its export-oriented industries to become more price competitive in those markets in an appropriate business environment. At the same time, reductions in Egypt's own barriers are enabling industries and households to acquire inputs at a reduced cost and thereby lower their production costs to become more competitive.

According to the GATT Secretariat, tariffs on industrial products imported by the industrialized countries from all sources will be lowered from a trade-weighted average of 6.4 percent to 4 percent as a result of the Uruguay Round negotiations; for industrial products imported by the industrialized countries from the developing countries (excluding the least-developed countries), the trade-weighted average tariff will be reduced from 6.8 percent to 4.6 percent.[4] These calculations, however, are based on ordinary tariffs, and therefore exclude products for which a Multi-Fiber Agreement (MFA) quota is the binding restraint. In those cases, the tariff-equivalent of the quota substantially exceeds the ordinary tariff. For Egypt, therefore, the percentage reductions in import barriers calculated on the basis of ordinary tariffs understate the true increase in market access resulting from the 1994 GATT agreements. Indeed, the average tariff-equivalent of binding MFA quotas, estimated by the GATT secretariat at 30 percent, is double the average ordinary tariff of 15 percent.

The overall trade effects of the 1994 GATT agreements are impressive. World trade is forecast to be about 12 percent higher by the year 2005 than it would otherwise be without the agreements.[5] The largest increases in trade are expected to occur in clothing and textiles. Trade in clothing is projected to be 60 percent higher, and trade in textiles is expected to be 34 percent higher than it would otherwise be without the agreements.

Egypt will not only benefit directly from the increased access to trade, but also from the larger trade resulting from higher income levels associated with the more efficient use of domestic resources when trade-related distortions are reduced or removed. Several studies have quantified the income effects resulting from the increased trade and competition in the world economy; these studies generally point to consistently high levels of income and employment as a result of GATT 1994. Estimates of the additional annual world income generated by the 1994 GATT agreements range from $213 billion to $274 billion.[6]

Notwithstanding these global generalizations, there is a clear need for additional analyses of the potential effects of the 1994 GATT agreements on narrowly defined industries in Egypt. The lack of competitiveness of many industries as a consequence of the current business environment could severely damage the progress that has been achieved in recent years in those industries. Consequently, improvements in the business environment must go hand in hand with the removal of the protection of industries, including the institution of appropriate antidumping measures within the rules of the GATT to counter the effects on industries being hurt by foreign dumping action.

The 1994 GATT agreements place special emphasis on the 'tariffication' of nontariff barriers (NTBs) to trade. For Egypt, the process of tariffication is well advanced, since under the IMF Extended Agreement, in effect since August 1993, Egypt has succeeded in removing many of its earlier quantitative restrictions. By the end of 1993, import bans were removed, except for those on textiles, garments and poultry, and additional or expanded NTBs to trade were prohibited. The import ban on poultry was to be removed by the end of 1994. An important exception, however, is the import restriction on textiles and clothing, which were not removed under the IMF Extended Agreement. The 1994 GATT agreements will require the elimination of those restrictions.

The agreement on textiles and clothing of GATT 1994 replaces the MFA, under which Egypt and other textile and clothing exporters have faced severe import quotas in the EU, the United States, Austria, Canada, Finland, and Norway. The effect has been a reallocation of production from developing countries toward industrialized country producers, with attendant inefficiencies. For Egypt, as well as other exporting countries, those inefficiencies have arisen from: 1) the reallocation of production from constrained exporting countries to domestic U.S. and EU suppliers; 2) the reallocation of production from previously unconstrained exporting countries to constrained exporting countries; 3) the reallocation of production from constrained exporting countries to currently unconstrained exporting countries; and 4) the inefficient allocation of production among firms in the constrained importing countries.[7]

The MFA has affected the exports of Egypt and other developing countries in different and often obtuse ways. In the EU market, the diversion of imports of yarns and fabrics from developing countries toward intra-EU trade remained fairly constant from MFA I in 1974 to MFA IV in 1986, at which point the import share of Egypt and other developing countries started to fall. In the United States, the rising share of imports of yarns and fabrics by Egypt and other developing countries were effectively arrested as of MFA I. In clothing, the share of Egypt and other developing countries in both U.S. and EU imports gradually leveled off in the successive rounds of MFAs and has stabilized in the last decade.

Under the 1994 GATT agreement on textiles and clothing, all MFA quotas will be gradually relaxed. Beginning in July 1995, quotas were removed on 16 percent of total imports; in 1998, an additional 17 percent of the restraints must be removed; and in 2002, another 18 percent of the restrictions will be removed. In this manner, successive reductions will achieve full relaxation of MFA-type restrictions by July 2005.

The GATT agreement on textiles and clothing has important implications for Egypt's exports, and it is important that further work be undertaken to examine its implications for exports during the transition period over which all remaining MFA quotas are to be removed. In particular, relaxation of quotas on Egypt and its competitors will have important implications for the ability or willingness of Egypt to compete for greater market shares in the U.S. and EU markets. Concurrent with developments in the global economy, the privatization and liberalization of Egypt's cotton production and of its spinning and weaving industries will undoubtedly alter production costs and competitiveness of these industries, and thereby offer an opportunity for Egypt to augment its export markets shares in those regions.

TOWARD AN INDUSTRIAL STRATEGY AND ACTION PLAN

The government has taken the lead in directing the economy away from state controls and toward competitive markets; and the public and private sectors are moving toward a common economic vision for the future—a commitment to competition and market liberalization, not just price liberalization, as the principal means of stimulating the economy toward more rapid growth and achieving higher living standards. But successful market liberalization will require far more rapid private investment in industry and its related services. For this to occur, major reforms in the institutional framework of the economy must continue to reduce the risk and raise the expected returns on manufacturing investment.

The private sector should continue to support government efforts to speed up institutional reform and to help it to identify the priority reforms to stimulate competition and new private investments; some are identified in this chapter. These aim to support the government's policies to reduce its role in production and shift it toward creating an effective business climate. In other words, the public sector would shift from direct industrial operation and control to the establishment and operation of a network of institutions that permit an effective market system. The public sector would focus on natural monopolies, such as bridges and roads, and areas where markets fail, such as in education, health, and environmental pollution. That would require supporting the public sector efforts to halt its continued microregulation and control over industry. Detailed regulation of entry, operation, and exit of firms, and time-consuming regulatory and taxation procedures should continue to be replaced by a system that simplifies business operations, within such limits as are consistent with the general welfare of the population.

This chapter has focused on a limited number of industrial constraint categories: implications of GATT for industrialization; the lack of enforcement of contracts; the definition and enforcement of property rights; other legal and judicial barriers preventing private firms from entering manufacturing markets; poor services from physical infrastructure like the Port of Alexandria; and other regulatory and administrative constraints. Other constraints to successful industrialization have been discussed throughout this book. With these impediments in focus, some recommendations for an action agenda for industrialization are presented below. The long-term industrial development strategy should be founded on three general principles: 1) the creation of a competitive market economy; 2) the improvement of the business environment in Egypt; and 3) the exploitation of new local, regional, and global opportunities.

GATT and the industrialization process

While considerable effort is being undertaken to study GATT, the need exists for a much more detailed understanding of the implications of the agreements for industrial sectors in the economy, and for the export markets of narrowly defined industrial sectors. Technical assistance should accordingly be directed to the analysis of the impact of the GATT world trade agreement in the following areas: the international competitiveness of Egyptian industries relative to competing suppliers to markets; the import demand in Egypt's foreign markets for narrowly defined industries in light of the ten-year phasing commitments; the growth of Egypt's exports in traditional and nontraditional manufacturing export markets, and changes in market shares resulting from increased competition with other suppliers; and the growth potential of foreign direct investment and of intra-industry and intra-firm trade.

The ultimate aim of this analysis should be to identify areas where technical support to industries could be used to develop Egypt's international competitiveness, increase intra-industry and intra-firm trade, expand foreign direct investment, and, where appropriate, develop new economic policies in light of the new GATT agreements governing trade.

Barriers to market creation

The public and private sectors should continue to work together to strengthen the laws impacting on basic property rights and enforcement of contracts. Work must be done to bring this all together into one legal package. A comprehensive review and modernization of the civil and commercial codes should be undertaken and implemented to provide the enabling legal framework needed for modern business and financial transactions in Egypt. At a minimum, these and other relevant laws, regulations, practices, and procedures should be amended in the following areas: first, a modern system of perfecting security interests and mortgages by all creditors—and not just banks—in all forms of property, including real property, personal property, and intangible property by simple registration of a security agreement in the Commercial Register; second, a modern system for equipment leasing in a manner that protects the lessor's interest in the leased property as against innocent third-party transferees fully and adequately by, for example, registration of equipment leases in the Commercial Register which would protect the lessor's interest by putting third parties on notice; third, provisions for other financial and commercial transactions in accordance with modern international commercial and financial practice; and fourth, replacement of the current system of exorbitant percentage fees for registering mortgages with a system of very low, flat fees such as LE50 for each feddan of mortgaged land to make credit less costly and more accessible to investors and businesses—especially smaller ones.

Barriers to entry—other legal and judicial obstacles

Legislation should be enacted, regulations promulgated, and official actions taken regarding investment in Egypt that would accomplish the following: 1) unify Egypt's confusing multiple investment regimes into a single system which will, to the extent possible, treat all investors equally whether Egyptian, Arab, or foreign; 2) replace the bureaucratic, multistep, and time-consuming investment approval process with the single step of registering an enterprise or company with the Commercial Register as discussed above, except for a few highly sensitive projects which could be specified on a short negative list; 3) channel public sector human and financial resources saved by streamlining the investment licensing and incentive approval process into investment promotion abroad and within Egypt, and into qualitative improvements in law enforcement, health, and the environment; and 4) undertake a review of the legal and procedural changes required to shorten the period to register an ordinary corporation, one not receiving incentives, to one week. Legislation is also needed to consolidate Laws 159, 230, and 203 into a unified business investment regime which excludes the Capital Market Authority and which separates listing from incorporation. The new unified business investment regime then needs to be made fully functional.

Barriers to entry and exit—public monopolies

The public sector's efforts to reduce the extent of monopolies by placing state-owned enterprises in different holding companies has not yet made them competitive. These firms still meet regularly to compare and exchange pricing and other information. In many existing industries, the small number of enterprises and their informal connections encourage collusion in price setting and distribution. In cases where there exists an effective public sector monopoly, the best solution is to privatize and to subsequently develop antitrust legislation to discourage collusion and encourage free entry of competitors.

Barriers to entry and exit—private monopolies

The public and private sectors should together study the appropriateness of enacting an antitrust law that would make noncompetitive behavior on the part of the private sector illegal. Barriers preventing competitive rivalry should be reduced. Antitrust enforcement is a response to the private-sector monopoly problem; its primary objective is to improve market performance by preserving and enhancing the natural competitive forces of the market place. A good understanding of antitrust enforcement requires knowledge of both the individual antitrust statutes and the agencies that enforce them.

It is time for us to start examining what institutional framework, or what variant of antitrust legislation, is appropriate to limit the extent of cartel behavior by firms operating in the Egyptian market. All existing laws and regulations relating to monopolies, anticompetitive business practices, unfair competition, and consumer protection should be thoroughly reviewed in light of Egyptian and international experience; comprehensive, modern legislation should be prepared accordingly.

Physical infrastructure

To enhance the efficiency and productivity of Egyptian exports, there is a need to demonopolize the following areas of port facilities and related services: shipping agencies, stevedoring of both cargo and containers, operation of bonded warehouses, general terminal dredging, and other services in the Port of Alexandria, the new port at Dekhalla, and Port Said. Similar problems exist with the airport facilities, and similar recommendations for demonopolization and privatization would lower the costs of transit trade.

The public and private sectors should work together to consider venues through which the private sector can penetrate the facilities at the Port of Alexandria. Privatization is not enough because a public monopoly could be replaced by a private monopoly, and the astronomically high prices of operating out of the Port of Alexandria would be unlikely to change. Private shippers argue that one solution would be to begin allowing the private sector to competitively provide all the port services.

Regulatory and bureaucratic environment

Losses in time, money, and business opportunities are the major effects of having to comply with the red tape inherent in the Egyptian regulatory environment. While the costs for licenses and registrations do not appear excessive when considered individually, collectively they are large. The licensing costs are important because in addition to the fees themselves, the costs represent fees incurred by hiring people whose responsibilities are dedicated to processing paperwork, or attorney and notary fees. Loss of time is especially apparent in the long waiting lines of public sector agencies, the lack of information and support organizations to facilitate the registration and licensing process, and the need to process forms in agencies located in different parts of the city.

The effects of public sector red tape are obvious in the case of lost business opportunity. Entrepreneurs could instead channel their time, energy, and money into generating new business, rather than coping with the required numerous regulations and licenses that serve as major obstacles to the profit-making objective of the private sector. Despite the fact that numerous licenses and registrations are necessary, many businesses operate without them. Small businesses are especially known to evade licensing procedures; they justify their noncompliance with these regulations by the prohibitively high cost of processing documents. Although this type of evasion does save time and money in the short term, it can ultimately force these businesses to confront the exact situation they were intending to avoid. Indeed, it could prevent the businesses from expanding in the marketplace due to lack of formal registration.

Proposals to reduce the amount of red tape need to focus on the reduction and elimination of certain regulations and formalities, and on the increased efficiency of public sector officials. Increasing public sector confidence in businesses is often a goal unto itself, as is fostering a working relationship between businesses and the state. Other possible lines of action include controlling corruption within the public sector, eliminating intermediary public sector agencies, and improving information available to the public.

In the case of internal constraints, regulatory reforms require a huge undertaking. The multiplicity of bottlenecks resulting from a cumbersome regulatory and bureaucratic system requires a comprehensive approach to understanding and remedying the problems inherent in such a system. Among the problems that need to be addressed as part of the reform process are the inadequate institutional framework, the absence of incentives to promote efficiency, and public sector involvement in the managerial decision-making process. Improvements in the present structure include concerted action in the following areas: 1) reform of labor laws to reduce government departments' interference with hiring and internal business relations with employees; 2) reform of the legal framework for securitization with respect to property rights and nonpossessory security interests on moveable property; 3) redirection of the legal system to apply punitive damages for noncompliance of regulations, and reduce ex ante enforcement methods through rules and regulations; and 4) reform of entry, operational, and exit rules and regulations.

In the case of external constraints, there remains considerable scope for continued reforms in trade and customs regulations affecting manufacturing exports. Taking into account the external constraints discussed earlier for private sector business activity, and in light of the new GATT global environment, the priority action areas should focus on the following initiatives: coordination of government agency policies, regulations, and fees; simplification of the drawback system, including the combination of repayment of customs duties and sales taxes together for refunds due under the drawback system, and enforcement of the tax-rebate system for all export items; development of a 'one-stop shop' for customs information and declaration to complete all export procedures related to customs, quality control, and agricultural quarantine; elimination of the monopoly of the public sector over port and airport services, and sanctioning of the private sector to engage in these activities; liberalization of Egyptian goods from any previous approvals required by any entity as regards quantity or price for nonbanned items; limitation of quality controls to products subject to health, sanitary, and religious requirements.

Protecting local industry from unfair trade practices

Within the framework of the Uruguay Round of GATT, Egypt must create, and adapt for its own use, the same trade practices as the developed countries including the United States and Japan as well as the nations of Europe. In other words, Egypt should emulate what the developed countries are doing to protect their domestic industries from unfair trading competition.

Specific policies to implement this strategy include protecting Egypt's industry from unfair competition, creating a business-friendly climate similar to those of our competitors, and supporting Egyptian industrial initiatives.

Protection of Egypt's industry from unfair competition

1. Smuggling and under-invoicing: Firms from some countries avoid paying customs duties or pay reduced customs duties, giving them a competitive advantage over Egyptian manufactures who must pay more for their imported equipment and raw materials. This kind of preferential treatment should be discontinued.
2. Dumping: The government of Egypt must proceed quickly to establish antidumping laws. This requires the training of staff, before trade liberalization takes place.
3. Adopt strict measures to insure safe and healthy imported products.
4. Upgrade Egypt's system of standards toward internationally accepted levels.

Create a business-friendly climate like those of foreign competitors

The Egyptian private sector supports the government's effort at liberalizing international trade. To compete effectively in international and local markets, our general business environment and operation costs should be similar to our competitor countries. Egyptian industry is now suffering from extraordinary costs associated with inefficient government monopolies. The Egyptian private sector is paying unnecessary costs for products and services provided by the public sector. These increase local production costs and reduce Egyptian competitiveness. The following costs could be dealt with in the following ways:

1. Cancel the 10 percent sales tax on machines and tools;
2. Cancel the 3 percent to 6 percent duty fees on all imported raw materials, machinery, and other imported industrial inputs;
3. Reduce or cancel the stamp tax;
4. Reduce the government selling price on industrial land in new industrial communities, or reduce their price increases for the next three years;
5. Remove government monopolies in services;
6. Reduce the approximately forty-five administrative steps and required signatures for importing and exporting goods in Egypt;
7. Establish an easy system for tax rebates to indirect exporters; for example, a small furniture exporter buys wood from a retailer, who buys from a wholesaler, who buys from an importer. The current system makes it impossible for this small exporter to receive his rebate on duties paid for the imported wood for the furniture he exports.

Supporting Egyptian industrial initiatives

To attract new investors, the government of Egypt should redesign its investment promotion incentives. In particular, it should provide grants for new investments in underdeveloped regions; reduce bank interest rates for firms that provide substantial new permanent jobs; provide tax holidays; subsidize land or leasing of government assets at a low nominal rate; subsidize or share training costs by paying a portion of the new employees' salaries; and finance industrial R&D.

Government policy has an important role in nurturing and reinforcing clusters, which are successful firms that are usually linked vertically through buyer and seller relationships, and horizontally through common customers, technologies, and marketing channels. When a cluster begins to form, the government can play a role in reinforcing it. Perhaps the most support can be provided through creating specialized factors, such as university technical institutes, training centers, data banks, and specialized infrastructure. Government policy will be far more likely to succeed in reinforcing an existing or nascent industry cluster than in trying to promote an entirely new one. Successful firms can often be identified by their ability to export, even in relatively small quantities.

Egyptian technology

Industrial development requires a steadily rising level of technology. New technology increases efficiency and commands higher prices through better quality. Technology pushes productivity growth. Stimulating technology, via R&D, is a widely accepted activity of all governments, because of its positive spill-over effects throughout any economy. For Egypt, the policy should focus initially on fostering innovation on commercial applications. Policies to stimulate commercial innovation go beyond promotion of science and technology, and include a wide variety of policies supporting competition. Programs should begin concentrating on technologies that affect old or new industries in which Egypt has an apparent competitive advantage. There should be an emphasis on research universities and not government laboratories. In many countries, diffusion of research is facilitated by the relative openness of the university. University research institutes can be more easily transformed into places where new businesses are formed, as professors and particularly students develop ideas with commercial potential.

Special emphasis should be placed on technology transfers and R&D through developing collaborative arrangements between research institutes and universities and the private sector. It is particularly important to forge strong links between research institutions and industry. The government cannot do this alone. The most important influence on innovation must come from the R&D efforts of the firms themselves. As mentioned elsewhere, the government can provide special incentives for encouraging company R&D spending.

Creating a national spirit in being able to compete globally

The government should encourage the general population to take pride in Egypt, and utilize this zeal to raise their productivity and improve the quality of their work. There is a need to associate "Egyptian-made" with quality. Egyptians should take pride in producing products that successfully compete in international markets.

1 World Bank, Arab Republic of Egypt. *The Private Sector Regulatory Environment,* Volumes I and II, Report No. 10049-Egypt, 1992.

2 For the purpose of industrial infrastructure, we include public utilities (power, telecommunications, piped water supply, sanitation and sewerage, solid waste collection and disposal, and piped gas), public works (roads and major dam and canal works, irrigation and drainage), and

other transport sectors (urban and interurban railways, urban transport, ports and waterways, and airports).

3 For details on the costs associated with these procedures and formalities, see the 1994 memorandum prepared jointly by FEI and the Ministry of Economics and Foreign Trade, *Ways to Simplify Export and Import Procedures and Reduce Their Costs*, and a May 8, 1994 FEI trade-related memorandum, *Extraordinary Costs Imposed on Egyptian Production and How to Deal With Them.*

4 GATT Secretariat, *An Analysis of the Proposed Uruguay Round Agreement, with Particular Emphasis on Aspects of Interest to Developing Economies*. Geneva, 1993.

5 Ibid.

6 I. Goidin, O. Knudsen, and D. vander Mensbrugghe, *Trade Liberalization: Global Economic Implications*. Paris: OECD and the World Bank, 1993; OECD, *Assessing the Effects of the Uruguay Round*. Paris, 1993; and GATT Secretariat, op. cit.

7 R. Faini, J. de Melo, and W. Takacs, *A Primer on the MFA Maze*. Washington, D.C.: Policy Research Working Paper No. 1088, The World Bank, 993.25.

Ten

Small and Micro Enterprises in Egypt

The Alexandrian Businessmen's Association

In the context of the Economic Reform and Structural Adjustment Program (ERSAP) that the Egyptian government has undertaken, private sector development (PSD) and industrial liberalization play a major role. Key to economic reform is a successful shift to a dynamic, market-based economy in which an unprotected and competitive private sector assumes the lead.

The public sector is currently the largest contributor to the gross domestic product (GDP) in Egypt. However, it is the private, small and micro enterprise (SME) sector that is the most promising for achieving broad-based, equitable growth in Egypt. SMEs are currently the largest private employer of the Egyptian labor force and contribute the most significant portion of the economy's private value added; nevertheless the sector is heavily restricted. With relatively few exceptions, SMEs do not have access to formal financial institutions, physical space, and/or regional markets.

CHARACTERISTICS AND ROLE OF SMEs

Small enterprises have been defined as those with between six and fifteen employees, while micro enterprises and rural development projects are defined as those with between one and five employees (Stearns 1992). In Egypt, the enterprises of this class share the following characteristics: 1) average asset level below LE5,000; 2) savings are the most common resource of start-up funding; 3) labor intensive; and 4) heavily concentrated in urban centers.

The majority of Egyptian SMEs are informal in that they are not licensed to be in operation. Nearly all SME operators are dependent on direct sales to their clients. Additionally, they are primarily directed to serve low-income consumers where low-quality, low-price products have a substantial market. Confusion and misunderstanding as to the correct definition of SMEs has resulted in a relative shortage of data and statistics concerning this sector; however, there is growing interest in Egypt, and numerous attempts have been made to measure the sector's importance to the economy.

Informal-sector enterprise unit counts based on official statistics include the following estimates: 876,000, the lowest estimate (Abdel-Fadil 1983); 1,104,300, referring only to working children between the ages of six and twelve (CAPMAS 1984); 3,000,000 (Rizq 1988); 2,280,621 (Charmes 1991). However, official figures often fall short of reality; this is because official counts ignore children (being employed) under the age of sixteen, itinerant workers, and low-income households. CAPMAS also undercounts the employed labor force holding second jobs in the SME sector.

Today, Egypt has a population of nearly 60 million people and a labor force of 15.9 million (the labor force being the segment of the population, employed and unemployed, from ages sixteen to sixty); of those 16 million people, SMEs employ nearly two-thirds, or around 11 million people (10.73 million, USAID-Cairo 1994).

Over the past decade, the Egyptian private sector has managed to absorb one out of every two entrants into the labor force. Approximately 60 percent of these new jobs were created by non-agricultural SMEs (Weidemann 1992). Within the private sector, nearly 90 percent of the registered establishments fall into the SME category.

The combined private sector in Egypt provided nearly two-thirds of the country's value added (61 percent) in fiscal year 1992, and 53 percent when agricultural outputs are excluded. The largest percentage of value added is produced by SMEs. The sector registers an impressive 80 percent of the total private value added (75 percent when agricultural outputs are excluded).

KEY CONSTRAINTS ON THE ESTABLISHMENT AND DEVELOPMENT OF SMEs IN EGYPT

Access to finance

The banking system in Egypt offers limited financing instruments to private enterprise. The longest terms of payment offered by banks on loans for the private sector is five years (the average loan matures in two-and-a-half years); SMEs generally receive more limited credit, if any. Credit is rarely given to certain sectors (e.g., mortgage markets), and consumer credit is still in the early stages of development. Local bankers attribute the reluctance to extend long-term credit to the lack of long-term project assessment capabilities, general macroeconomics uncertainty, and the high cost of collateral recovery (caused by the poor state of the commercial judicial system). Similarly, lack of competitive pressure in the banking industry as well as inflexible collateral requirements keep local banks away from the SME lending business. As a result, Egypt's banks concentrate on short-term commercial lending to medium-sized and large companies.

Access to physical space

Location factors play an extremely important role in determining the concentration of SME subsector activities and their potential for economic and financial viability. Key determinants include urban–rural linkages (commodity flows and marketplace fluctuations), local population concentrations, transportation infrastructure (railroad, bus, and road access and services), and market infrastructure, such as warehousing facilities.

For SMEs to operate effectively, they have to be located near densely populated areas. In this way, they can have easier access to labor; be closer to the markets they serve; and reduce the need for, and costs of, transport.

Access to markets

The demand for goods and services produced by SMEs is derived from four sources: 1) the domestic demand for consumer goods and services stemming from the incomes of households; 2) the backward and forward production and distribution linkages between SMEs and other producing units of the domestic economy; 3) the government and public sector; and 4) export markets.

Clearly, the primary demand for SME goods and services in Egypt lies within the domestic market, and particularly among low-income households (Liedholm and Mead 1987). Yet intersectoral linkages are strong only in the forward linkages from agriculture to SME production and service activities, which are reflected in food processing, transport, machinery maintenance and marketing services (e.g., packaging, point of sale). Backward linkages, from large- and medium-scale enterprises are more rare, while government procurement rules are practically impenetrable to SMEs, as are export markets, especially because of the country's lack of large international trading houses.

Access to technology

'Evolutionary' changes in products and/or services and technology/design will continue to be a major threat to the survival of the small-scale enterprises. Unless SMEs have access to technology and research and development (R&D), their lifetimes will be very short. This directs us to the problem of SME integration. Management and market potential depend on the skills of the operator, and include organizational capacity, access to information, and market surveys; they are referred to as internal factors. Yet few institutional mechanisms exist in Egypt to provide SMEs with technology, management, and information support.

SUCCESSFUL EXPERIENCES IN ESTABLISHMENT, SUSTAINABILITY, AND GROWTH OF SMEs

Bangladesh's Grameen Bank

The Bangladesh experience with SMEs represents a very successful case in the area of rural development. This achievement has been facilitated by the establishment of Grameen Bank.

Grameen Bank began as an action research project under the patronage of Bangladesh Kirshi Bank. Through this bank, more than a million formerly very poor rural households in Bangladesh have improved their living standards significantly. The bank's approach toward achieving this involves disbursement of small loans, exclusively to the lowest-income rural households, to finance additional income-generating activities at reasonable terms, requiring neither collateral nor guarantors.

Korean experience with medium- and small-scale enterprise

The last thirty years have witnessed a change in the attitudes toward SMEs in Korea, due mostly to a general realization of their major role in adding vitality to the economy. The Korean government has taken rigorous steps toward the promotion of SMEs, including:

1. Establishment of NGOs solely for SMEs: the Korean Federation of Small Business, the SME Institute, and the SME Promotion Organization have all facilitated the development of comprehensive promotional policies and systematic financial assistance for SMEs.

2. Establishment of the Industrial Bank of Korea specialized in giving financial assistance to SMEs.
3. Establishment of the Korean Credit Guarantee Federation to extend guarantees for the liabilities of promising business enterprises which lack tangible collateral to obtain funds from financial institutions.
4. Promotion of cooperative activities among SMEs; for that purpose the government enacted the Small Business Cooperative Act in December 1961.
5. Promotion of SME exports; in accordance with this plan, 350 SMEs have been designated as potential exporters and have been provided with various incentives designed to strengthen their international competitiveness. In selecting the eligible firms, priority was given to those demonstrating prospects for increased export volume, strong foreign exchange earnings, and efficient use of existing facilities.
6. Establishment of industrial estates to provide accommodations for, and to ensure economies of scale for, export-oriented SMEs.

USAID-Cairo

In 1989, USAID-Cairo entered into cooperative agreements with two NGOs: the Alexandria Business Association (ABA/SME) Foundation and The Cairo Foundation. The foundations provide small loans (averaging LE2,300 for working capital and equipment) to SMEs at commercial rates of interest. The loans are of short-term duration, usually between eight and eighteen months. In four years of lending in Cairo and Alexandria, through just six branch offices, the foundations have provided over thirty thousand loans (including return customers) of LE77.4 million to their SME clients. On-time repayment rates exceed 97 percent.

In August 1992, the National Bank for Development (NBD), a non-profit private Egyptian bank, negotiated the 'Greater Cairo' effort with USAID, known as the Small Enterprise Credit Program (SECP). In twelve months of lending activity, through thirteen NBD branches, NBD made 20,205 loans (including return clients), for a cumulative total of nearly LE45 million. Loan processing is simple and loans are processed in a matter of days for first-time borrowers, and are nearly automatic for return, on-time paying clients. Rates of interest are market-determined, traditional banking collateral or security is not required, and 10 percent of the required loan amount is deposited as savings with the bank.

RECOMMENDATIONS

The following are policy suggestions for SME development in Egypt, as seen from the local private-sector point of view:

1) Offer incentives and more relaxed terms for the establishment of banks who are willing to specialize in funding SMEs.

2) Establish an SME Promotion Fund, financed by contributions from the government and business associations, loans, profits yielded by its operation, and grants from donor countries, and managed by a board of directors representing the business community and SME experts. It should be used to carry out the following activities: modernization projects; facilitating business conversion projects; cooperation projects; career/employment guidance and training projects; fostering rural small industry and the indigenous craft industry; investment in business to support vulnerable enterprises and commercialize new technology; development and introduction of technology by small entrepreneurs; start-up assistance for SMEs; leasing facilities for the projects; collecting, disseminating, investigating, and researching information; and providing subsidies (if necessary) to enhance/encourage the success of the above activities.

3) Extend the activities of the public sector–owned Principal Bank for Development and Agricultural Credit to those in rural areas who are not covered by the traditional banking system.

4) Establish a Small and Micro Enterprises Council. The council would be composed of not more than twenty members from public and private businesses with knowledge of and experience in SMEs, and should be chaired by the Minister of Public Enterprise. The council should be authorized to formulate policies to: facilitate the development of SMEs; train business managers; establish and expand research institutes for technology implementation; formulate standards and inspect goods to improve the quality of goods and services provided by the SMEs; improve the working conditions of the SMEs; promote subcontracting between large enterprises, medium-sized enterprises, and the SMEs, and rationalize subcontract conditions; establish a mutual aid system for SMEs so that they can avoid bankruptcy through mutual aid; establish orderly export transactions and open markets abroad; improve the system for tendering government bids in order to offer more opportunities for SMEs.

5) Governorates and donors, utilizing qualified business associations, should support the establishment of industrial estates/parks close to the metropolitan areas, as was done in Korea. As a pilot project, the Egyptian government might allocate lands for industrial use to be developed and administered by business associations for

SME industrial parks. Special funds should be made available by the donors to provide necessary infrastructures, shell-factory buildings, and estate management facilities for these properties.

6) Governorates should reconsider granting licenses to SMEs locating in urban areas, which do not pose threats to the environment.

7) Business associations should be encouraged to play a role in providing SME entrepreneurs with, among other things: information on local and international markets and their prospects; market access by providing exhibition outlets to market their products; technical assistance and training on an industry basis; help in developing contacts between SMEs and middle- and large-scale industry/business; help in acquiring necessary skills and know-how for preparing and entering into contracts and/or subcontracts, through contract management training.

8) Set an agreed-upon model of industrial establishments that will satisfy all the necessary conditions, and free SMEs from licensing and other bureaucratic proceedures.

9) Business associations and NGOs should provide workshops to be attended by SME clients and led by local authorities to explain the establishment and operation of licensing, social insurance application, and the institution of laws. This would further the understanding of the laws and increase compliance.

10) Establish small-business development centers in rural areas to stimulate and provide support for new and existing businesses. These centers are to be managed by governorates representatives, business associations, and NGOs. They can assist by providing information and ideas for SME projects; by providing land, premises, and leasehold arrangements; by providing the services of professional business advisors in technical, financial, legal, marketing, and managerial matters; by offering joint buying and selling services; and by providing management and manpower training facilities.

11) A fiscally neutral approach needs to be formulated and applied that widens the SME tax base, while allowing lower marginal tax rates.

12) On the global level, pressure the international institutions and developed nation donors to establish an international bank for microenterprise development to provide finance on a large scale to small lenders in the developing countries.

BIBLIOGRAPHY

Carl Bro International. "Small and Micro Enterprise Development in Aswan and Qena Governorates." Draft presented to the Ministry of Foreign Affairs, Cairo: January 1992.

Easterly, W. *Explaining Miracles*. Policy research working paper, World Bank, February, 1994.

Fahmy, Randa and Ferando Gruz-Villalba. *Other Donor Projects in SME Sector*. EQI/NCBA, Cairo: 27 January 1994.

Gibbson, D.S. et al. *Banking on Rural Poor*. Grameen Bank, February 1991.

Hossain, M. *The Impact of Grameen Bank on Women's Involvement in Productive Activities*. Grameen Bank, November 1984.

Industrial Bank of Korea. *Small and Medium Enterprises in Korea: Their Legal Underpinnings*. December 1993.

Industrial Bank of Korea. *Small and Medium Industry Policies in the Korean Economy*. 1992.

Kilany, E.M. *Small Scale Industries in Egypt*. National Planning Institute, Cairo: June 1992.

Martin, W. *What Would Happen If All Developing Countries Expanded Their Manufactured Exports?* Policy research working paper, World Bank, 1993.

Middle East Times. "Social Development Fund Weathers its Growing Pains." April 1994, p. 6.

Shams, M.K. *The Grameen Bank Experience*. Grameen Bank, April 1992.

Shuhabulddin, R. *The Impact of Grameen Bank in Bangladesh*. Grameen Bank, September 1992.

Stearns K. "Small and Micro Enterprise Development Project No. 262-0212 Egypt", GEMINI Technical Report No. 30, March 1992.

Tucker W. *USAID Egypt: Small and Micro Enterprise Country Program Strategy*. USAID-Cairo, April 1994.

Weidemann C. and Z. Merabet, "Egyptian Women and Microenterprise: The Invisible Entrepreneurs." GEMINI Technical Report No. 34, Bethesda, MD: Development Alternatives, Inc., March 1992.

World Bank. *Egypt Financial Policy for Adjustment and Growth*. September 1993.

World Bank. *Social Indicators of Development*. 1993.

Notes on Contributors

Marcelo Giugale is a senior economist in the World Bank's Baltics Department, and until 1995 was both the World Bank's senior resident economist in Egypt and a professor of economics at the American University in Cairo.

Hamed Mobarak is the director of the Civil Service Reform Unit, Government of Egypt, and the secretary of Egypt's Private Sector Development Committee.

Caio Koch-Weser is Vice-President for the MENA Region, the World Bank.

Ibrahim Shihata is Vice-President and General Counsel, the World Bank.

Hussein Ibrachy runs a private law practice in Cairo specializing in corporate law. He is currently the chairman of the Economic Legislation Committee of the Egyptian Businessmen's Association.

Hazem Hassan is chairman of an accounting firm in Egypt. He is a member of the Government Audit Organization and of the Accounting Standards Setting Board of the Central Bank of Egypt.